CENTRAL MIDDLESEX (WHERE THERE MAY BE VERY LITTLE OF *IT*, BUT *ARE* MANY NICE PEOPLE AND PLACES TO SEE)—VA, & A STRANGE DÉJÀ VU: A Photographic Essay

Volume 2 of 4

Allen R. Brockman

CONTENTS

FOREWARD to Volume 2

As noted in Volume 1, of Central Middlesex (where there may be very little of *it*, but *are* many nice people and places to see)—Va, & a strange déjà vu: a photographic essay, Middlesex County is located in the eastern part of the State of Virginia and borders the Chesapeake Bay. This photo essay focuses merely on the central portion of the County—where it is the most interesting and the author/photographer lives. The County Seat is Saluda. Other than in supporting sections, such as this one, the author intentionally kept the text to a minimum. Poignant photos speak for themselves, but have been captioned for the sight-challenged, where necessary or for those Yankees who may be less familiar with our County and have yet to retire to our shores and links.

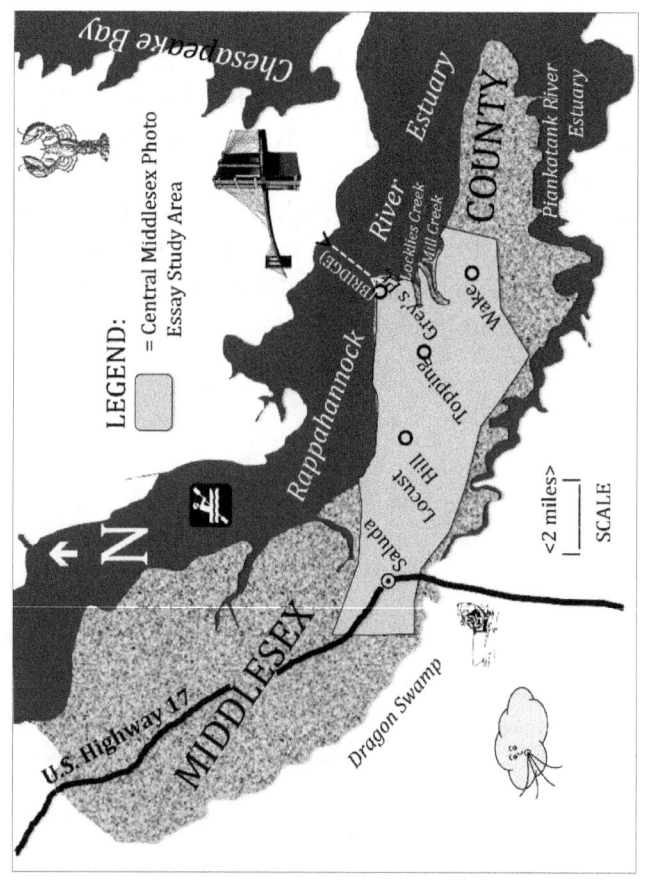

COINCIDENTALS, LIMITS ON THE AUTHOR'S ENDORSEMENTS, AND DISCLAIMERS IN THIS BOOK

Other than the generally alphabetical ordering of the business and restaurant photos, the relative sequence of the photos merely is for the reader's logical convenience and is in no way meant to imply that any of the Middlesex people in the juxtaposed photographs endorse each other or any controversial position which may appear to be endorsed by the author. Any such appearances are merely coincidental, the author assures you.

Some of the photos in this book captured images that were easily accessible from the public right of way and/or captured billboard messages or other signs about a County property, which easily are accessible—from public thoroughfares, to any county resident who chooses to make a general circuit of the County's roads. However, where the photos might require closer access and permission, and/or where the photos were of individuals, the author contacted the property owner and/or the property owner's representative and each person pictured in the photo. The author explained to them the general anticipated character of this book, where they would be able to locate both the book (once published) and the author.

Finally, after snapping each shot, the author reviewed the image with those pictured, asked for any information they would like to give the reader, and the author obtained their permission to publish their likeness(es) in the book. Any appearance of endorsement of any political or religious view by anyone pictured in the following pages is purely coincidental and has no factual basis. In fact, even the author has no clue about what any of these folks believe about such issues. Nor does the author's family, who *does* know the author, either necessarily agree with any opinions herein, explicit or implicit, nor should they! So please give them a break.

In turn, the author has chosen the folks pictured because he has been satisfied with their business services and endorses them from what he experienced on past occasions under their roofs. So stop by and see them, ya hear?! But the reader is cautioned against accepting the author's recommendations, herein, as any sort of express or implied warranty. For such warranties only can be proffered by the respective merchants themselves—not by the author. The author's liability, if any exists, springs forth only from the fact that you risked buying this book.

PHOTO SECTIONS AND CHAPTERS—

Section III—ANIMALS (of all kinds & places):

CHAPTER FOUR

Interesting Animals—or <u>for them</u>

The Animal Lady of Saluda (Dr. Adine Jones):

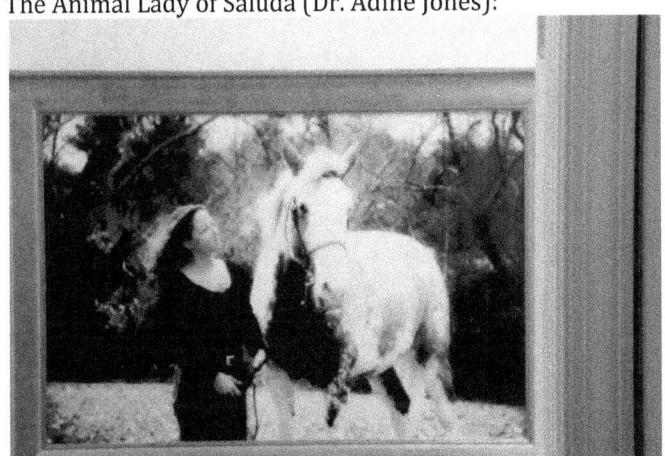

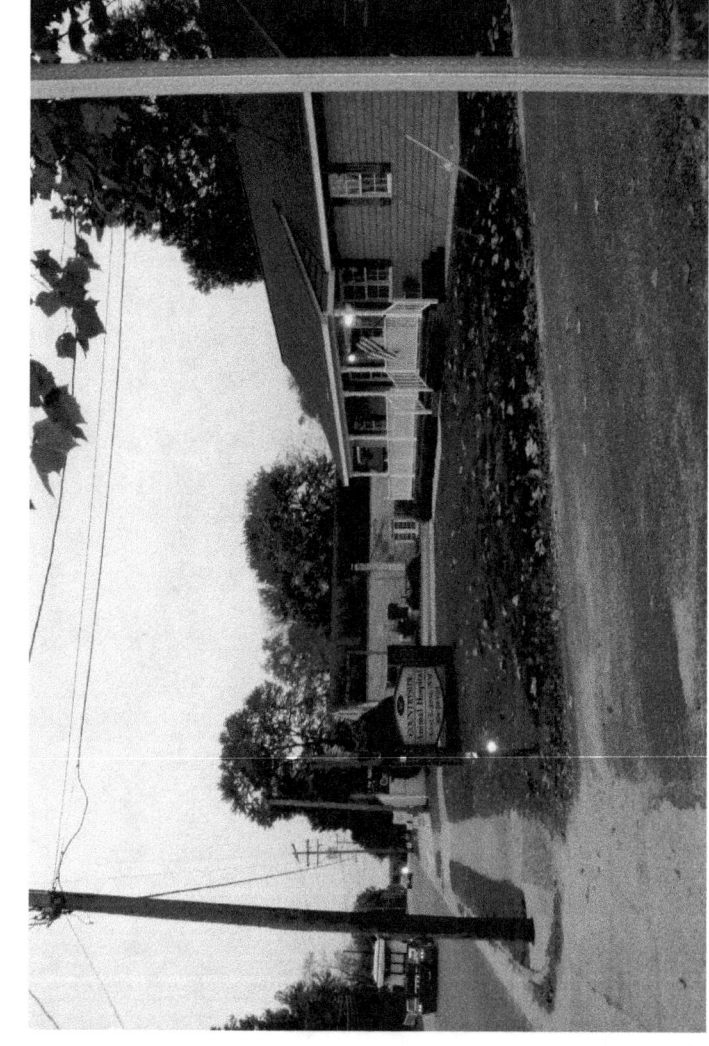

Dr. Jones's place of business is at 507 Gloucester Rd.

10

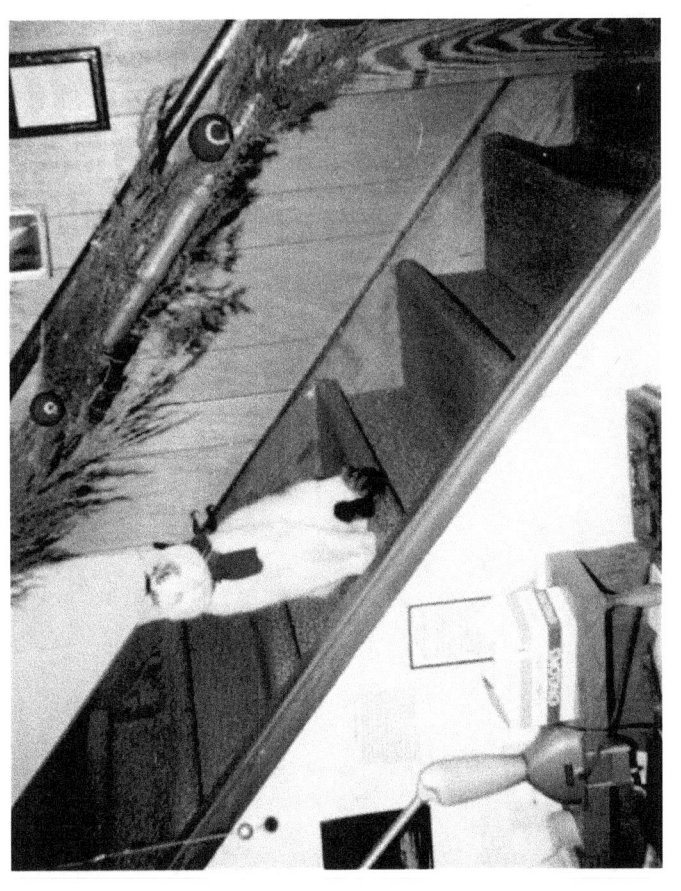

11

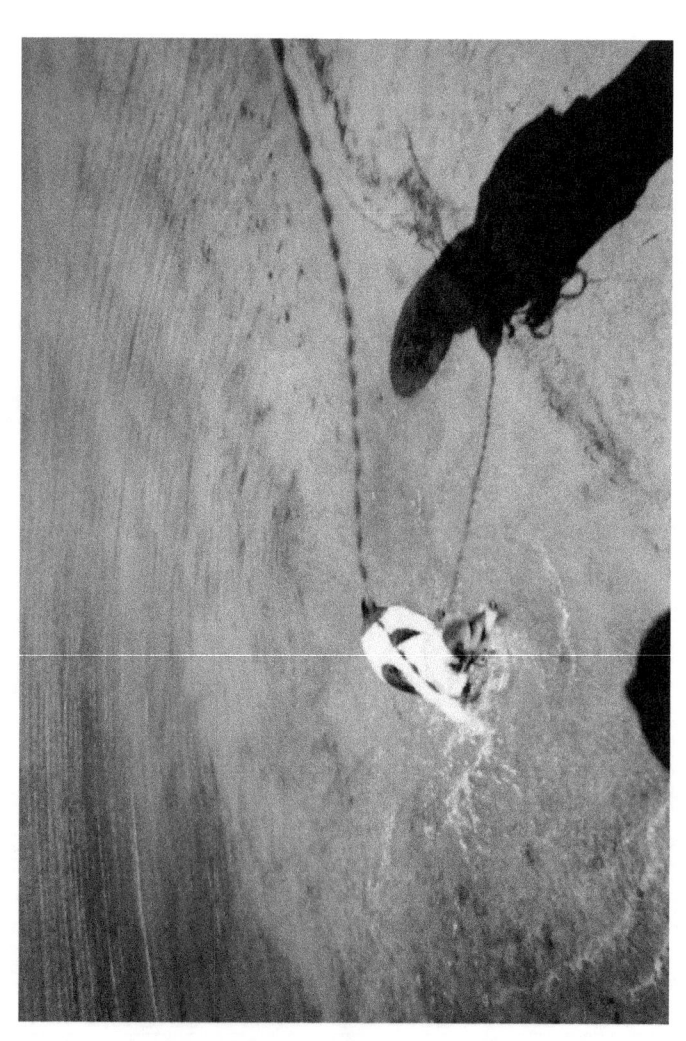

12

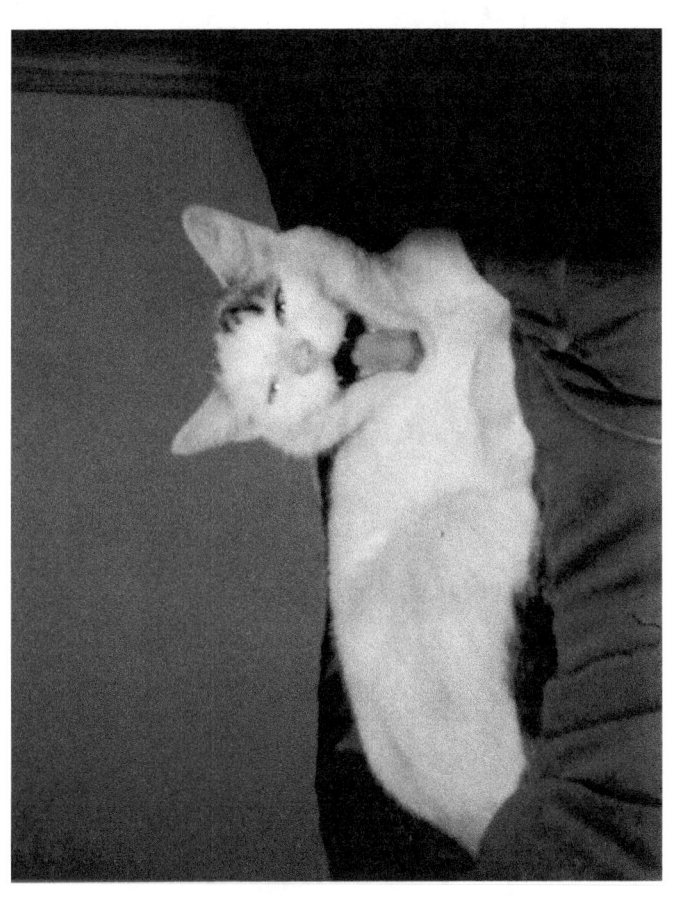

13

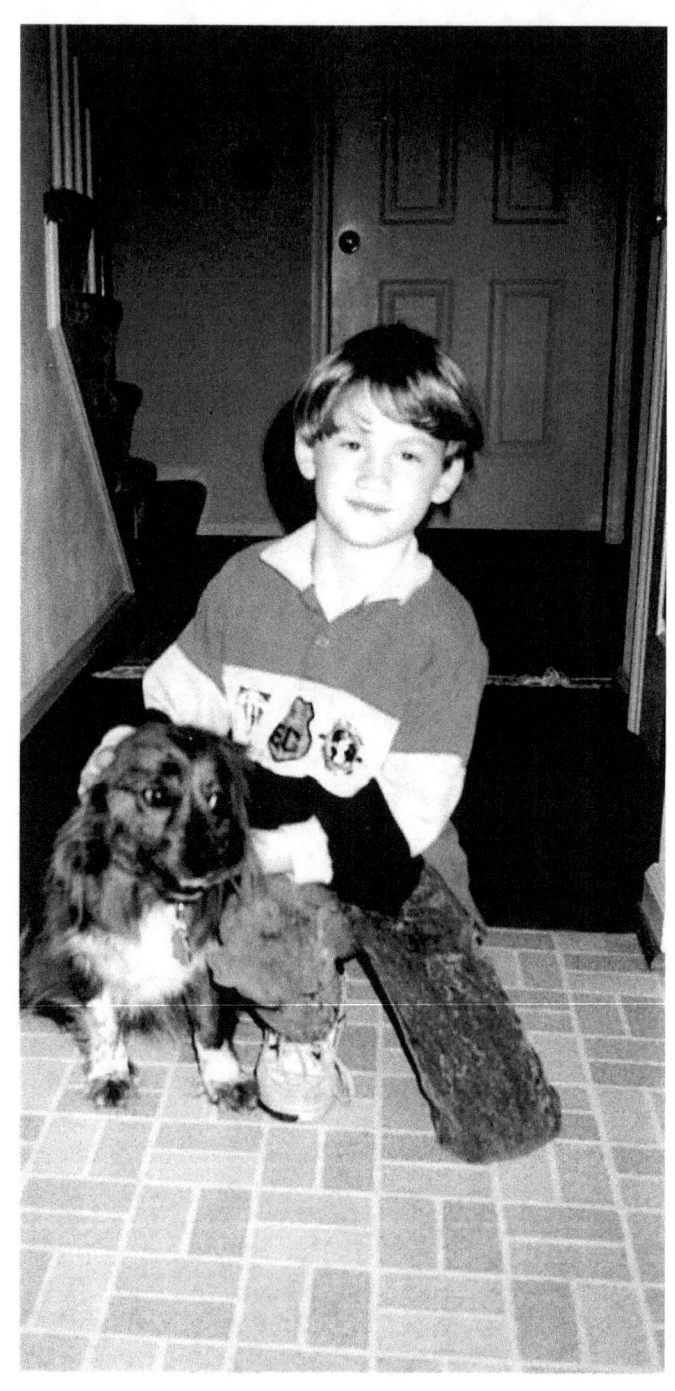

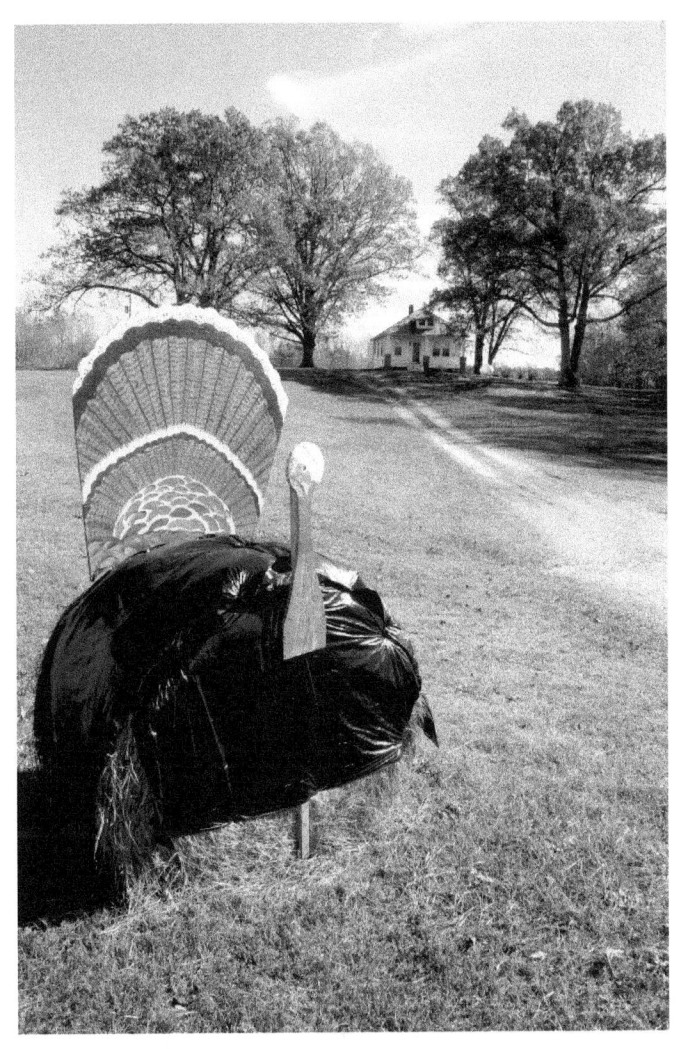

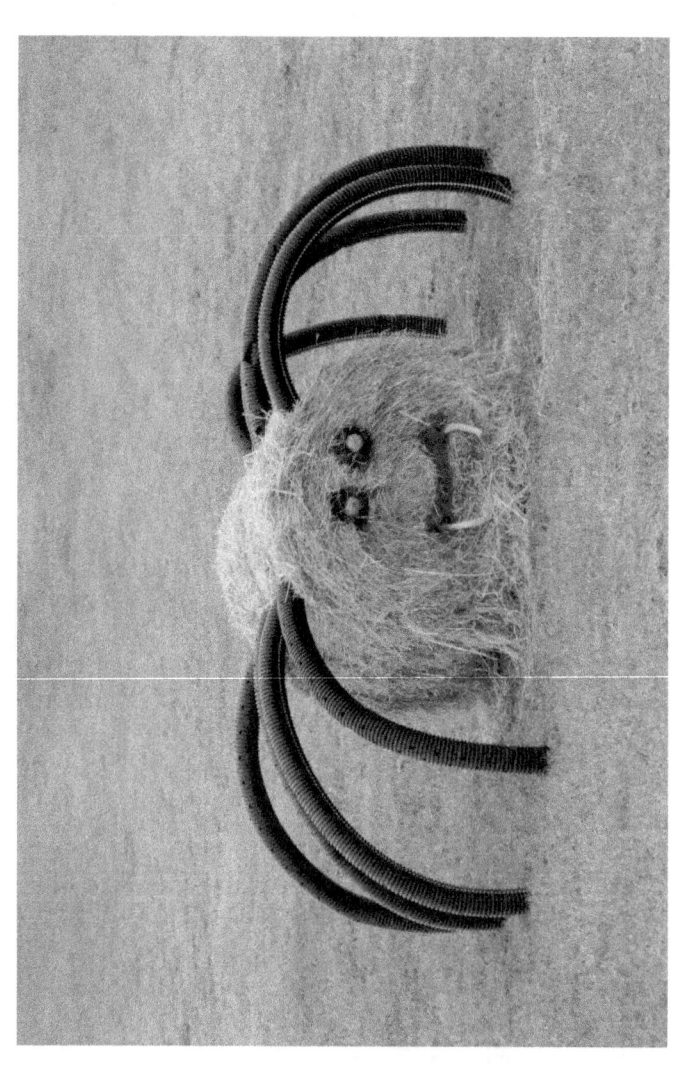

16

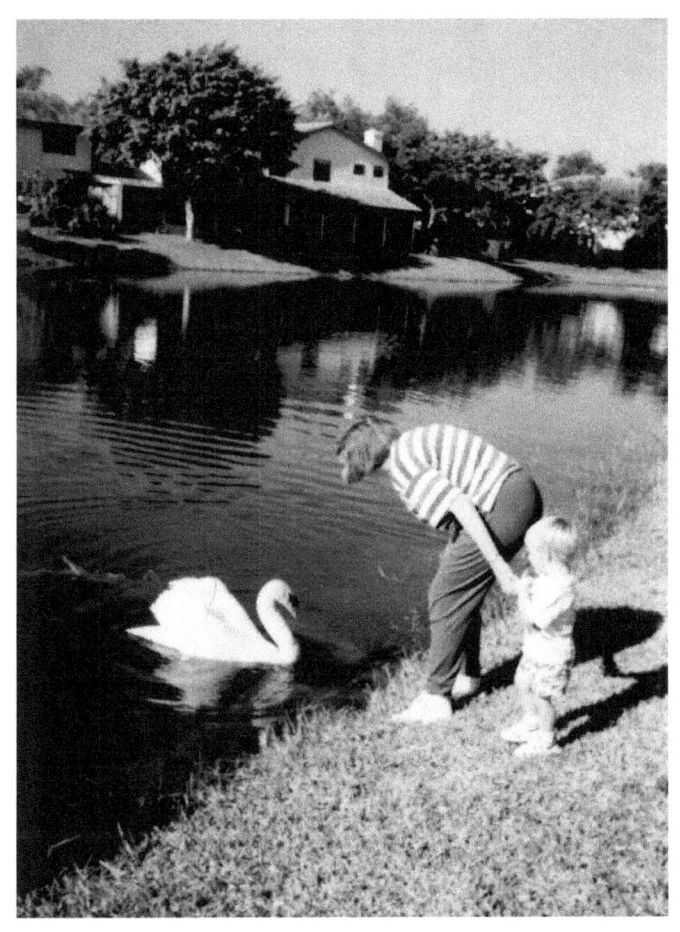

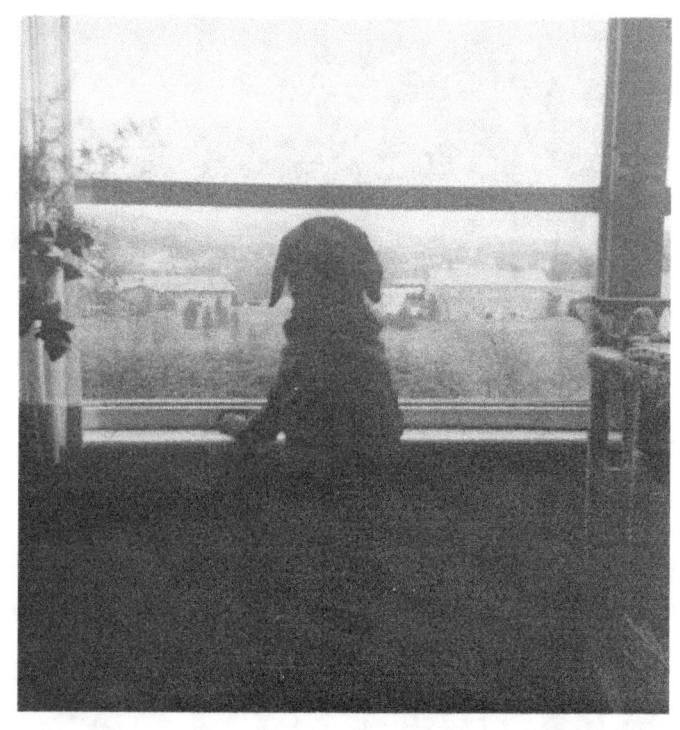

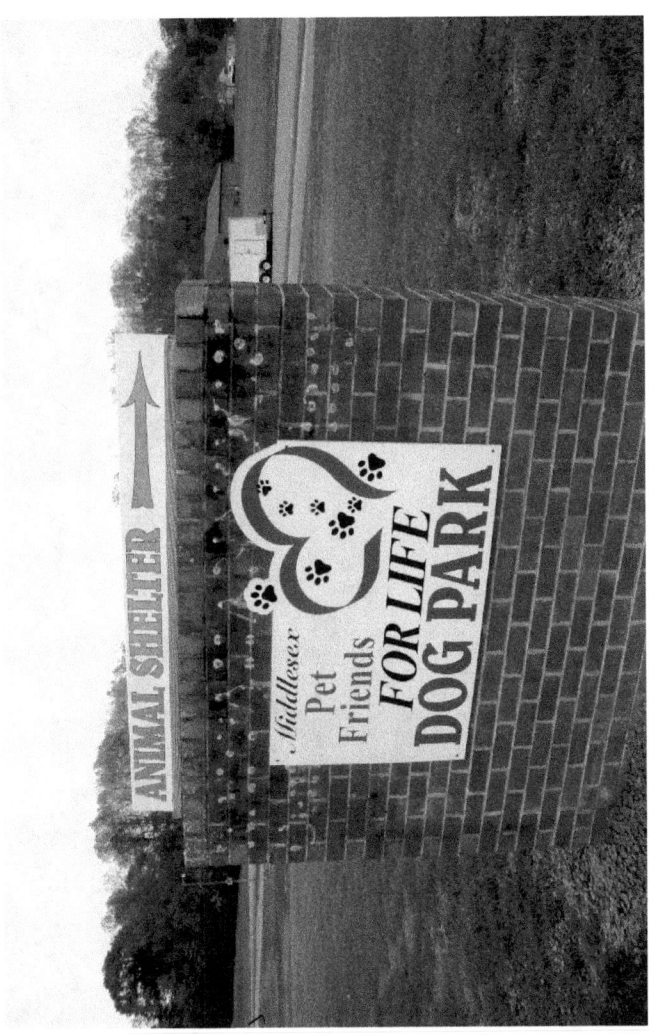

ANIMAL SHELTER

Middlesex
Pet
Friends
FOR LIFE
DOG PARK

Horses
along
Wake Rd

Horse
Boarding
on
Stormont
Rd near
Saluda

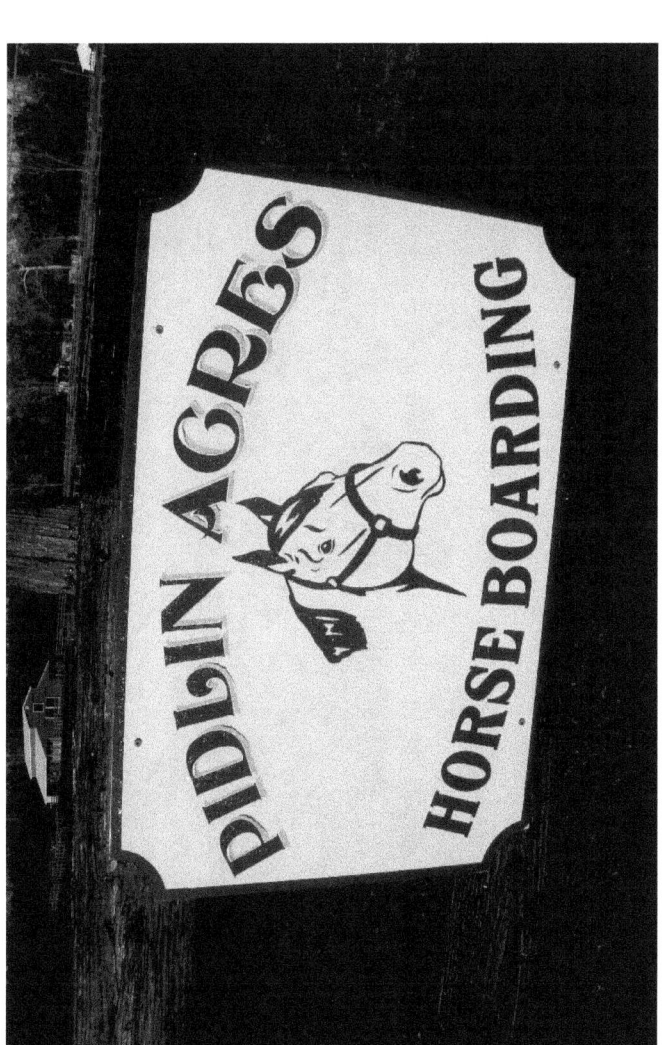

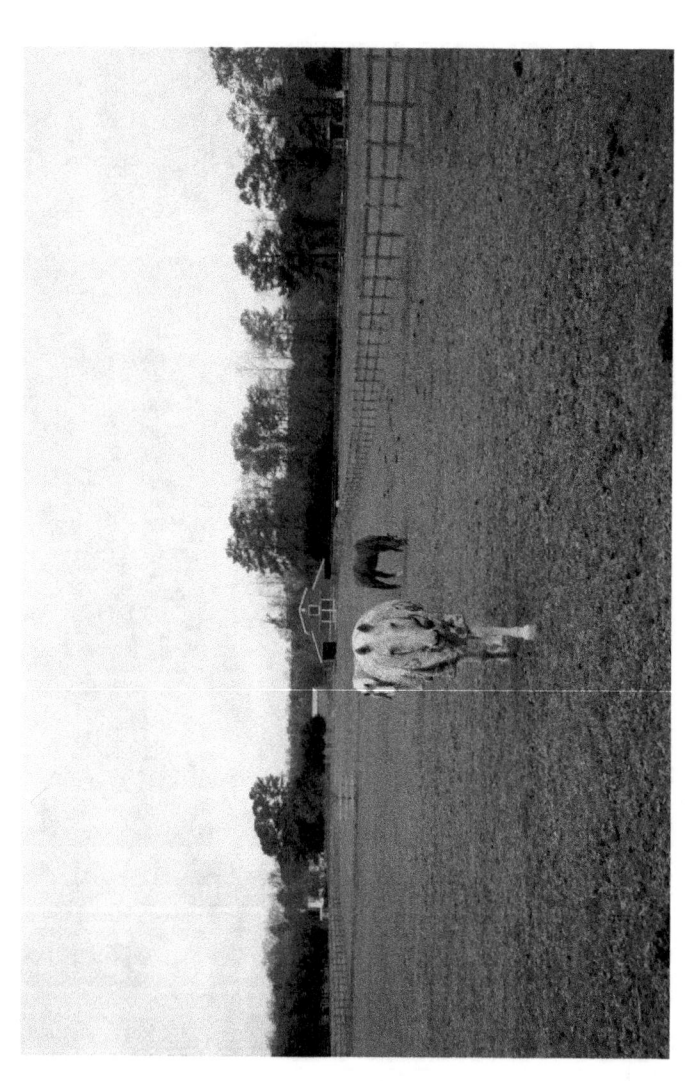

22

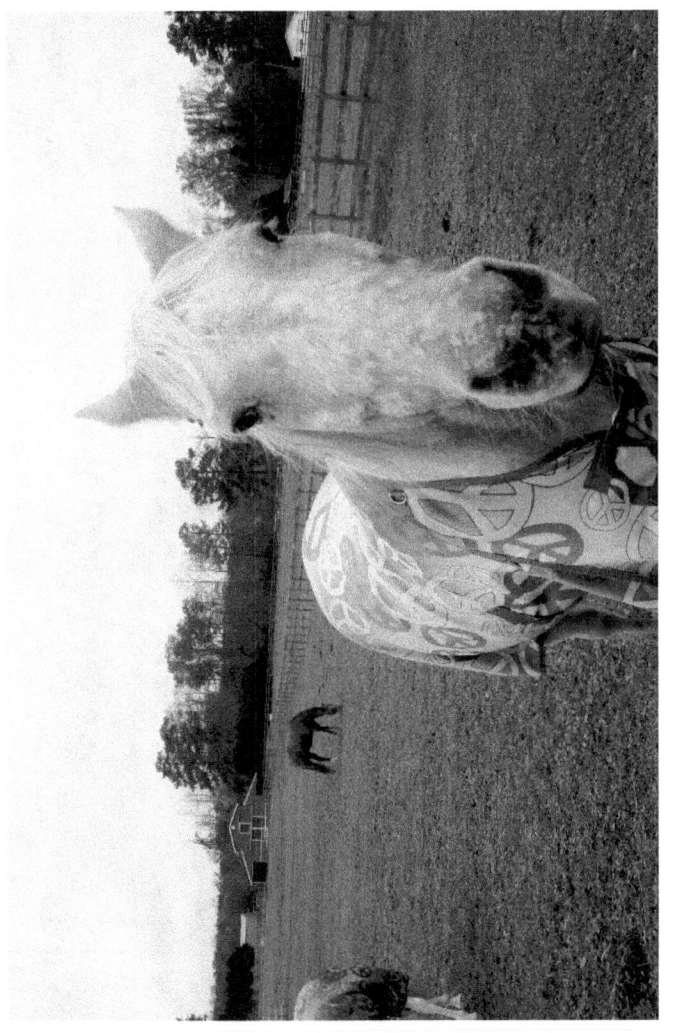

23

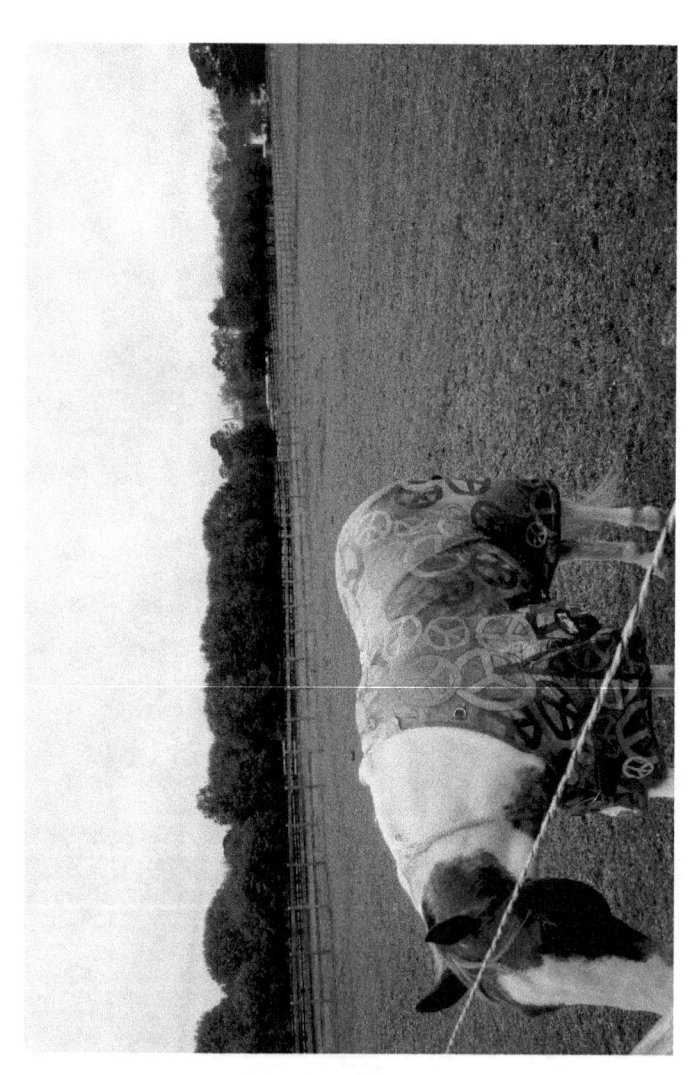

24

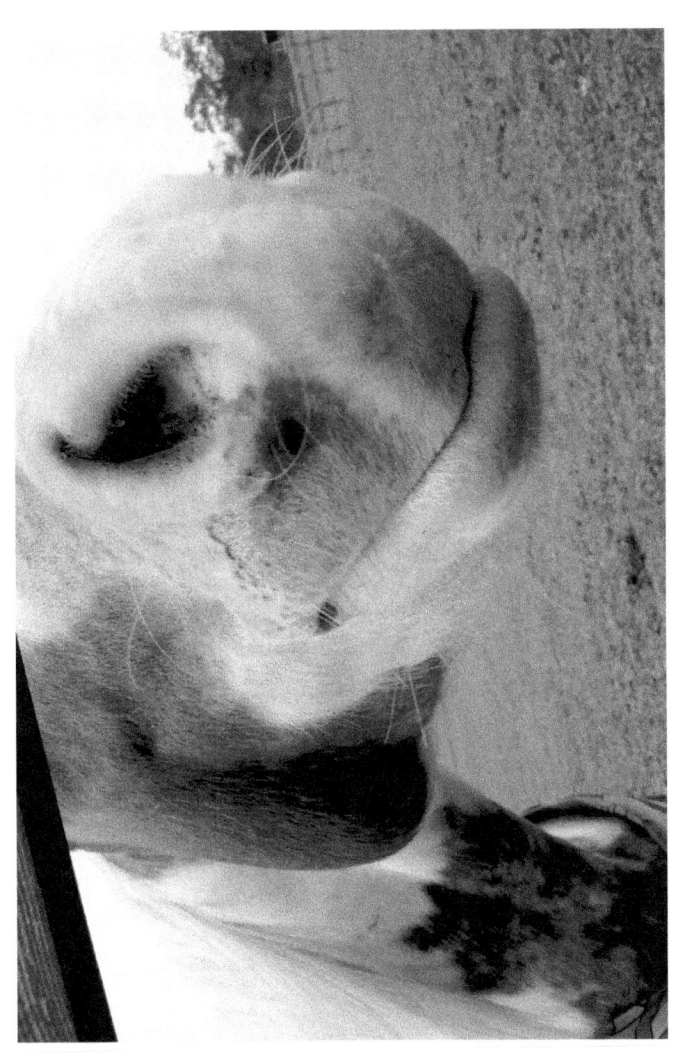

25

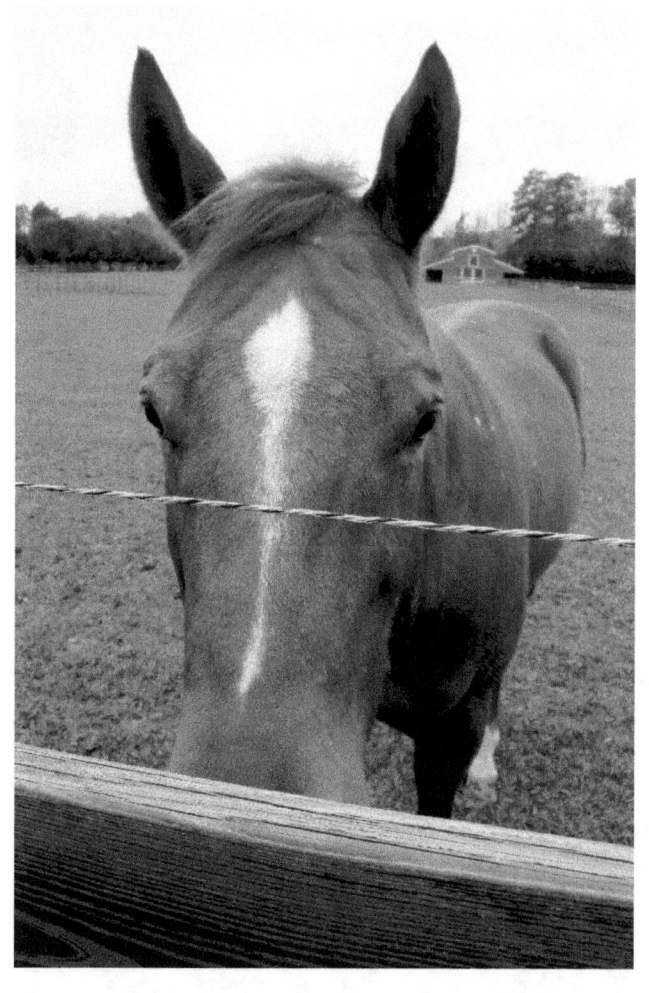

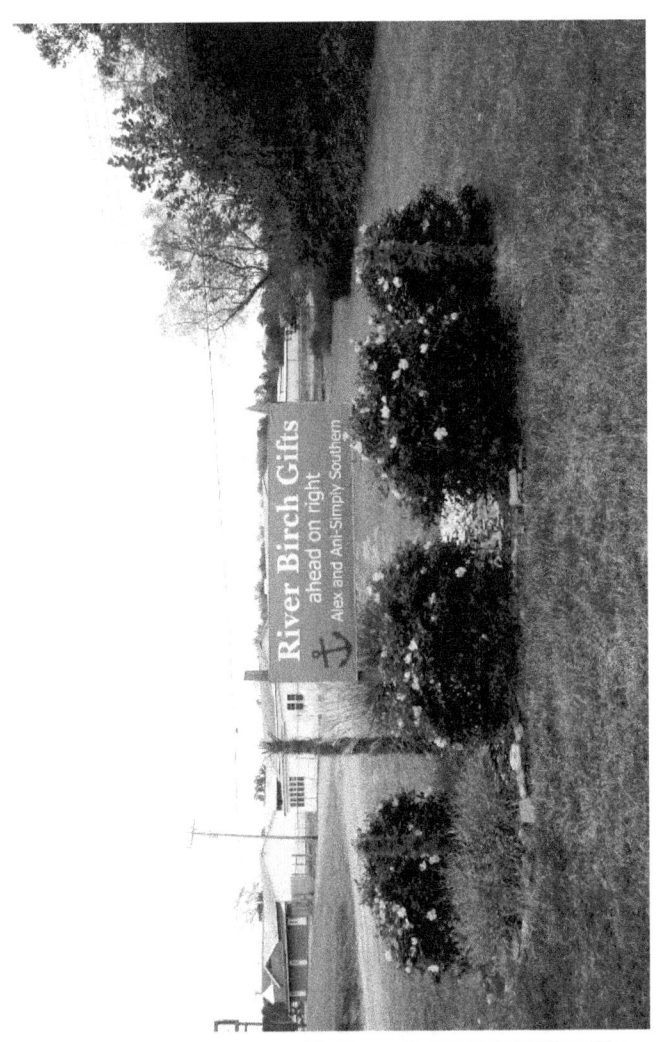

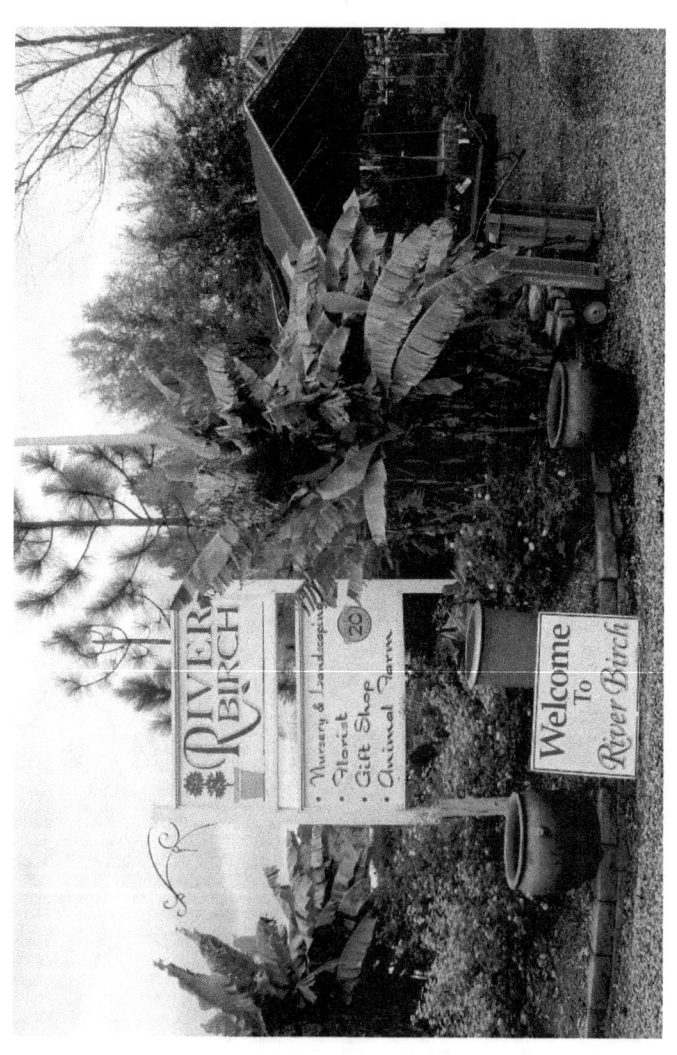

28

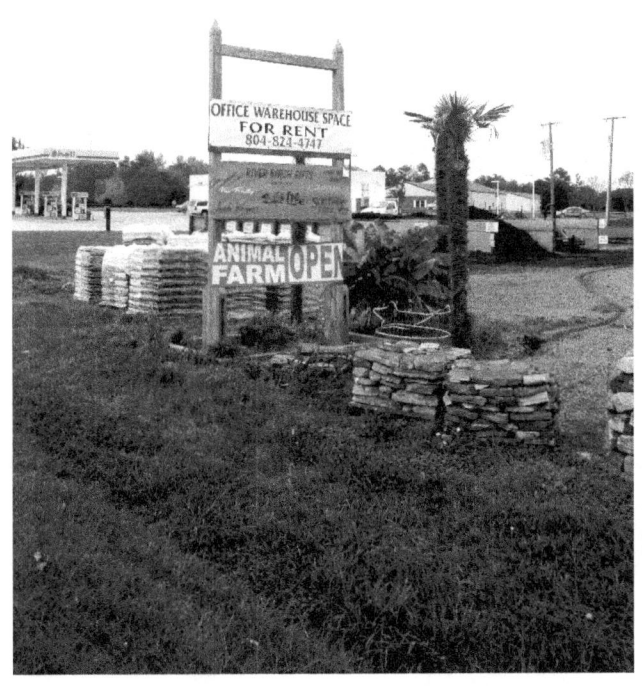

From here to the dead opossum, near the end of volume 1, all of the rest of the animals are from the River Birch Animal Farm.

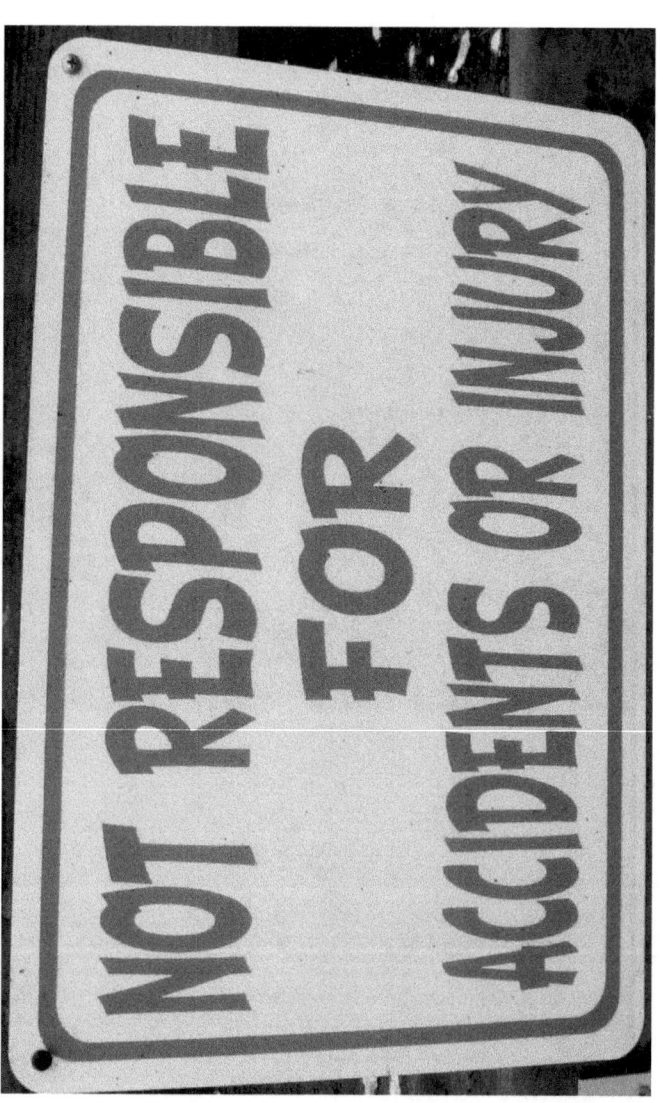

(I promised Mr. Major the baby donkey would be the star of volume 1--also, my wife is a *Jenni*, too, so the baby gets **19** photos)

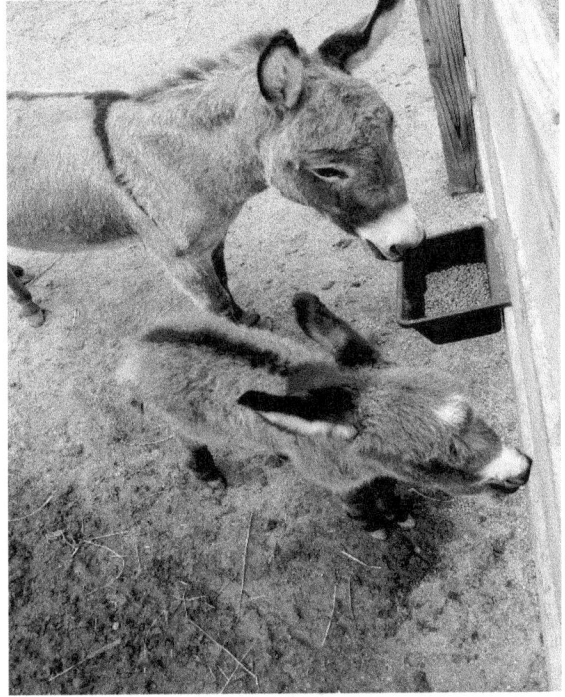

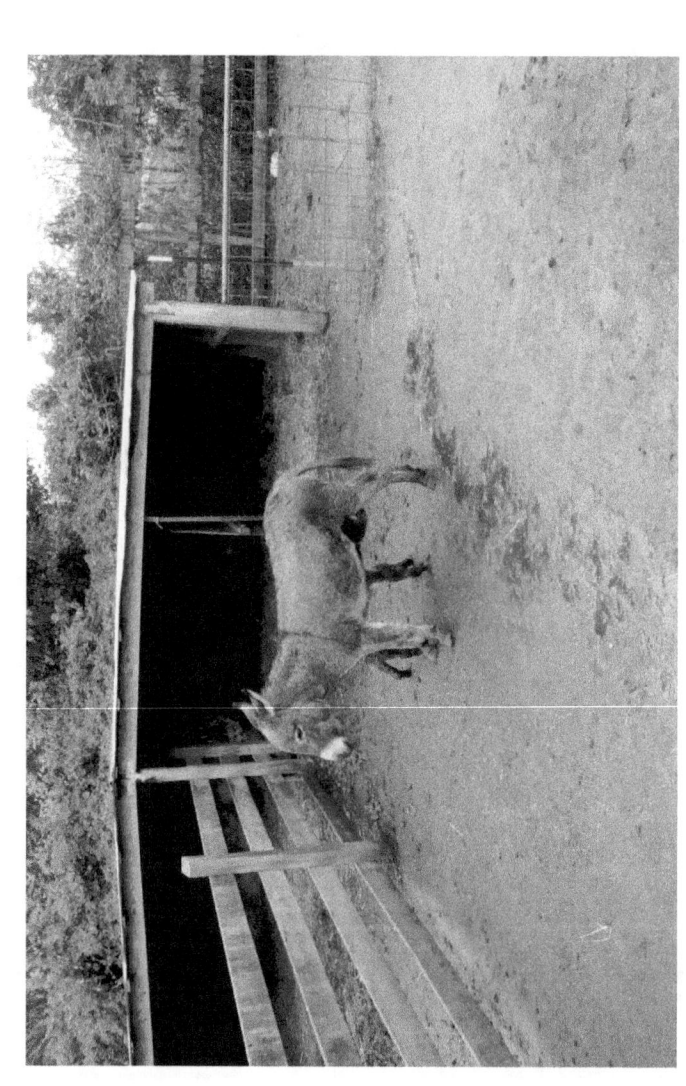

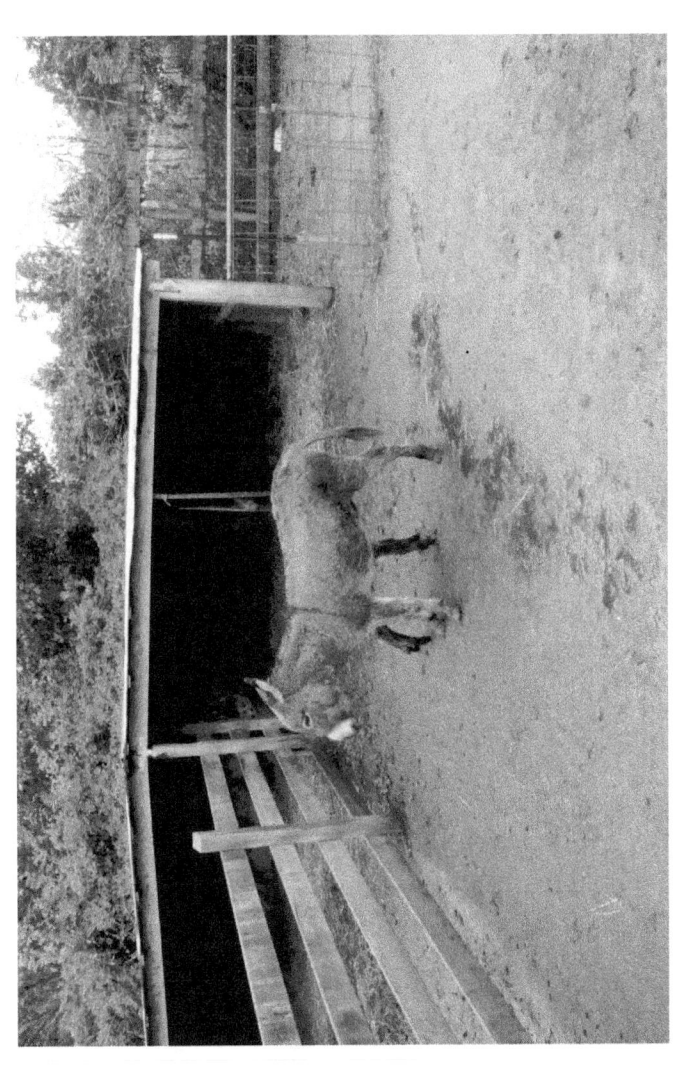

33

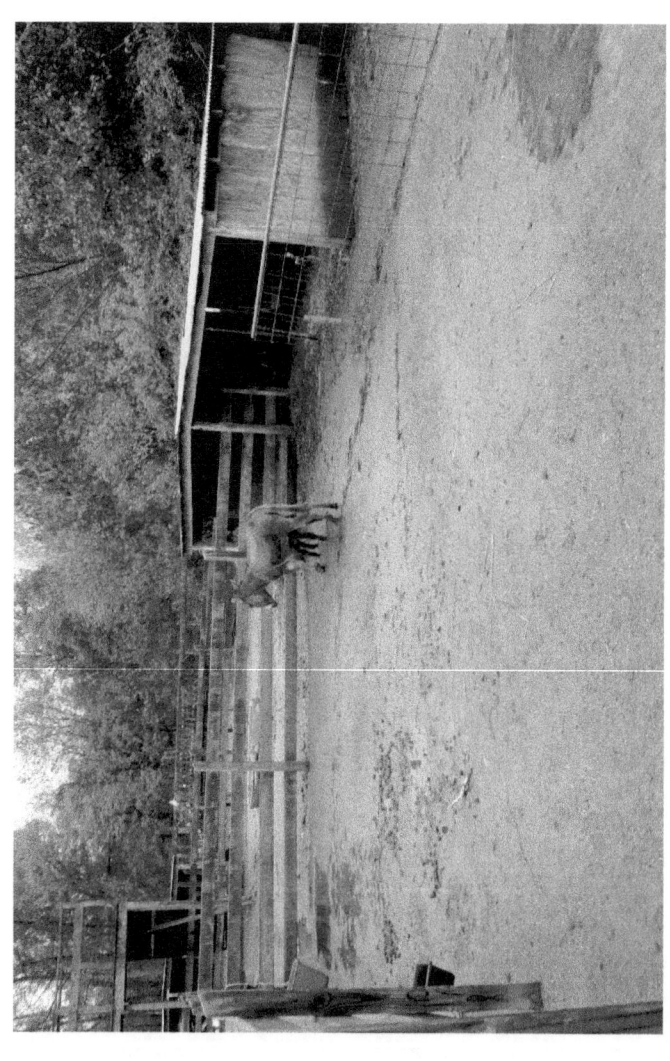

34

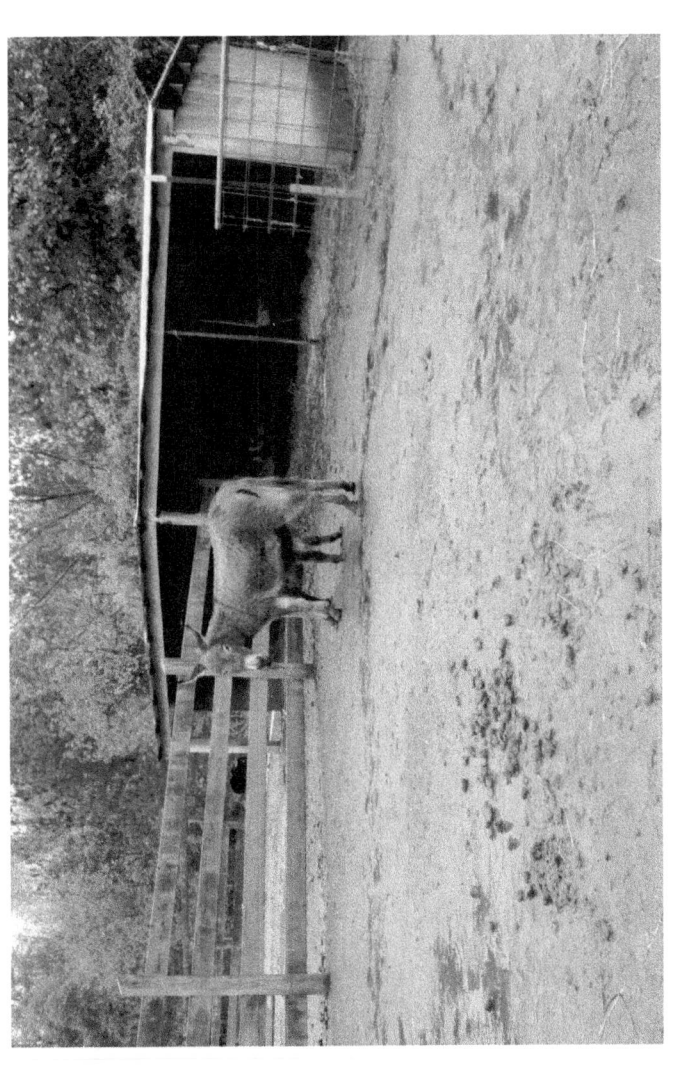

35

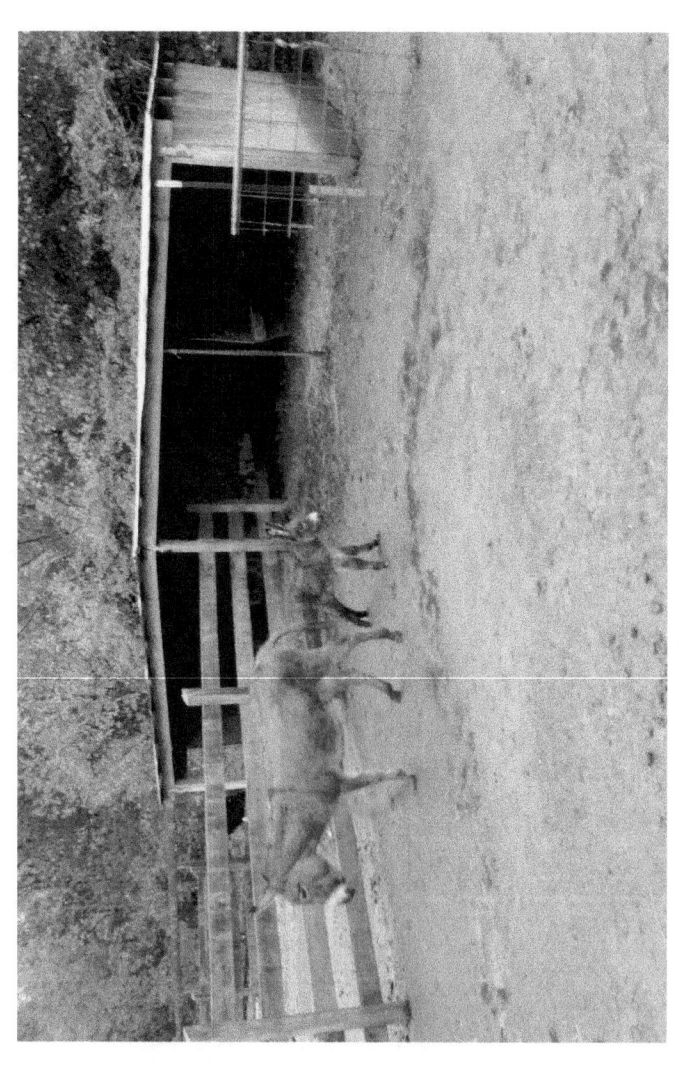

36

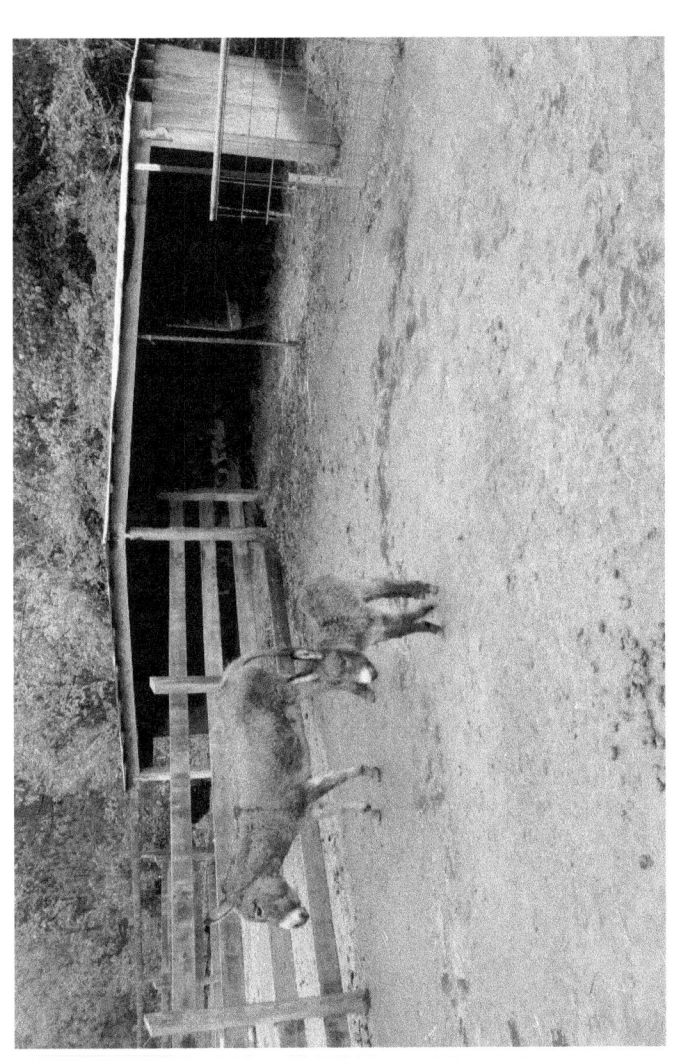

37

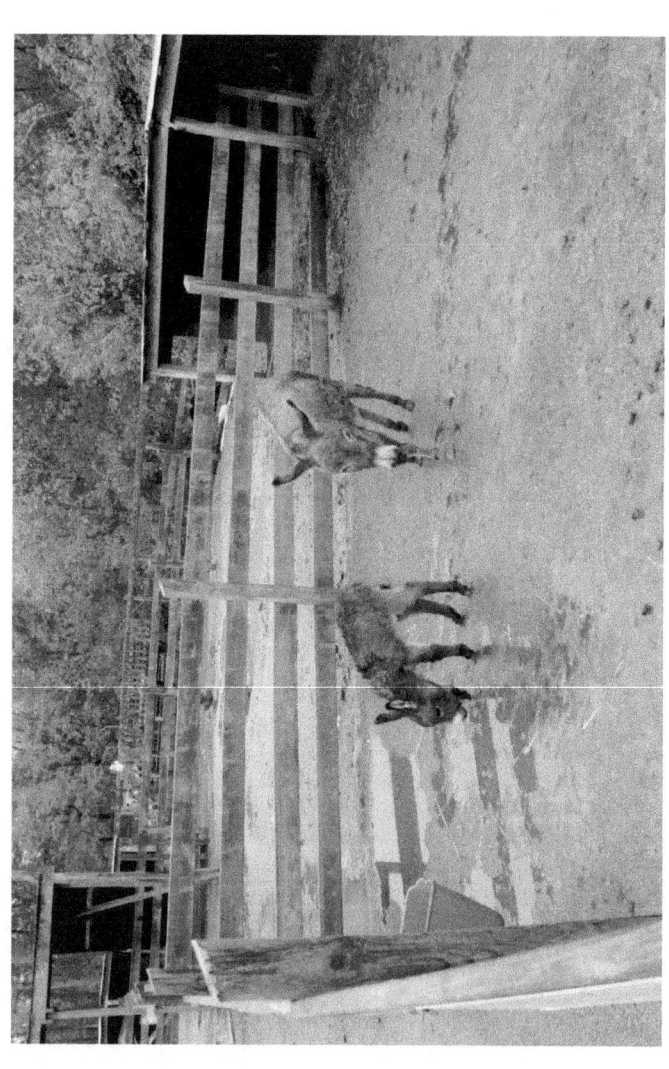

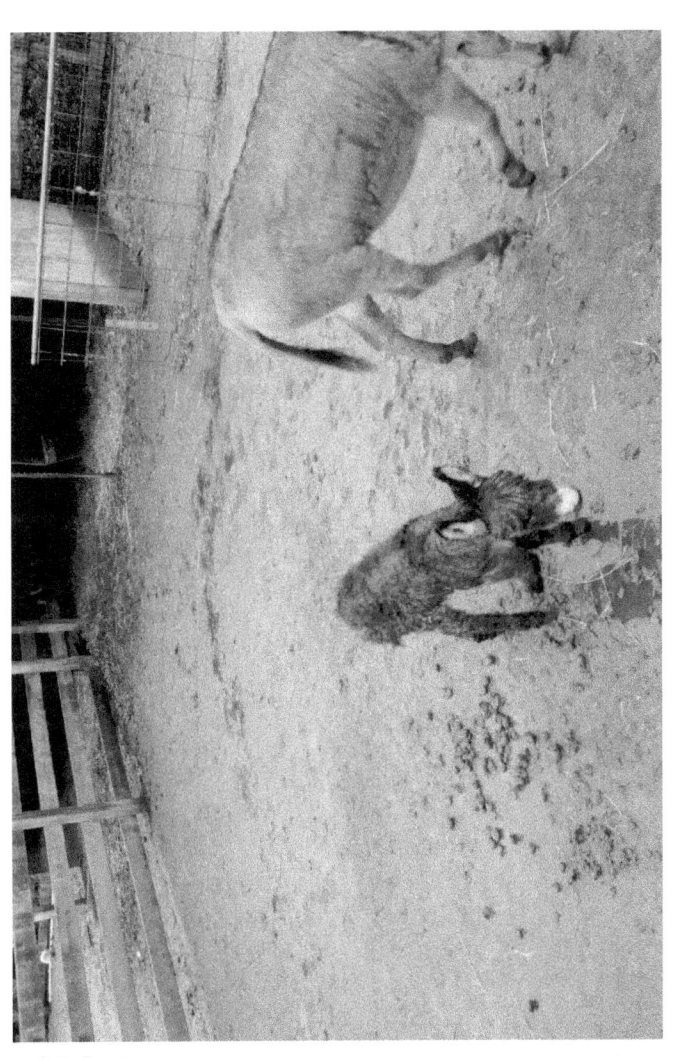

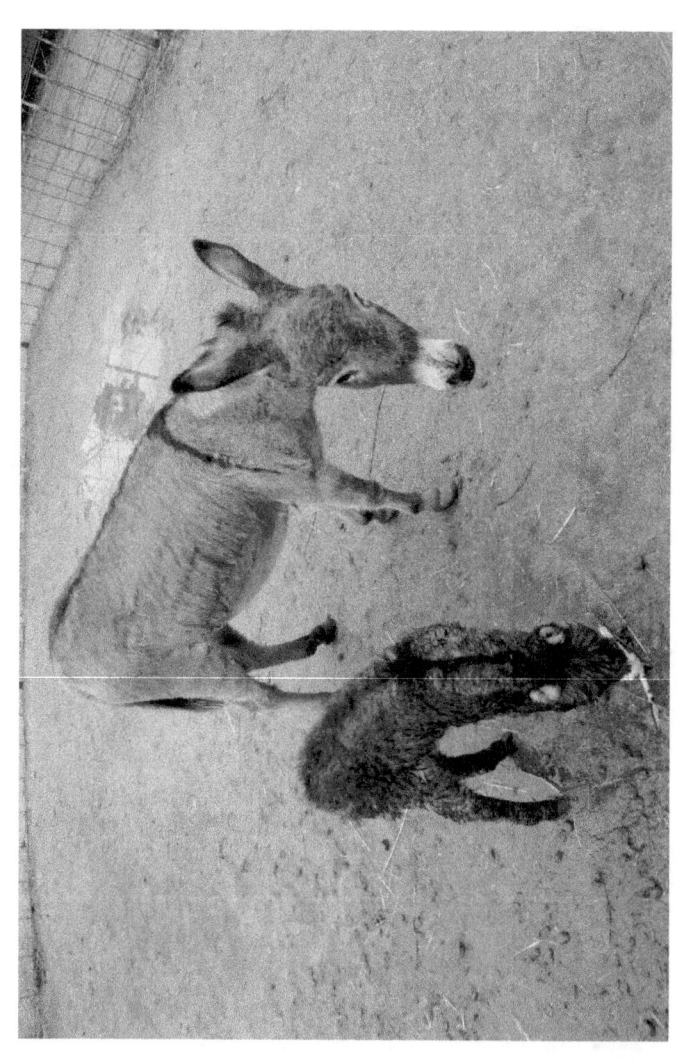

40

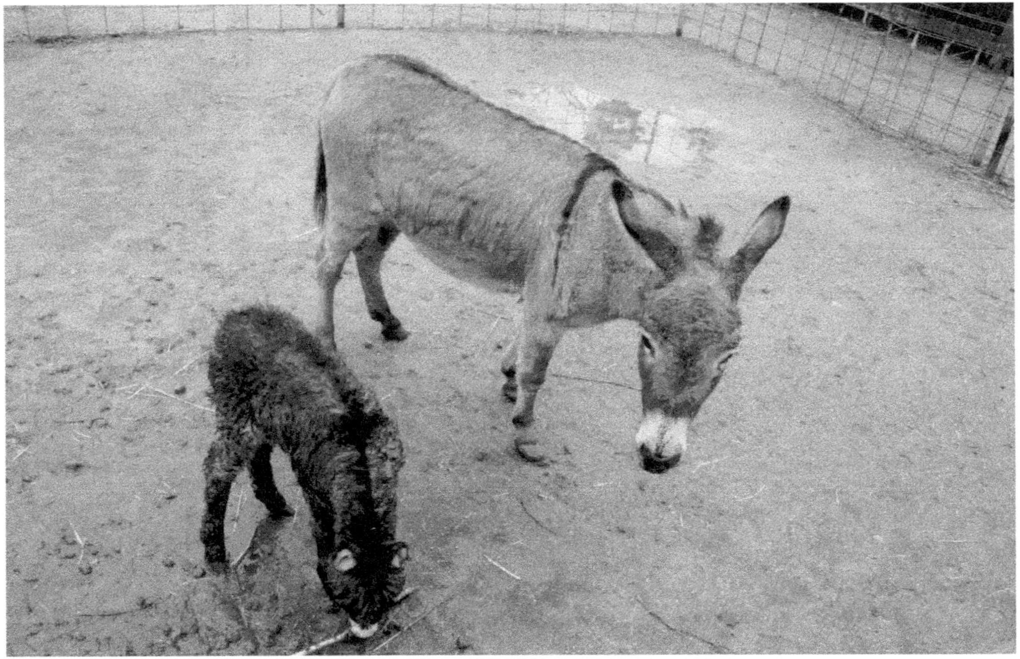

41

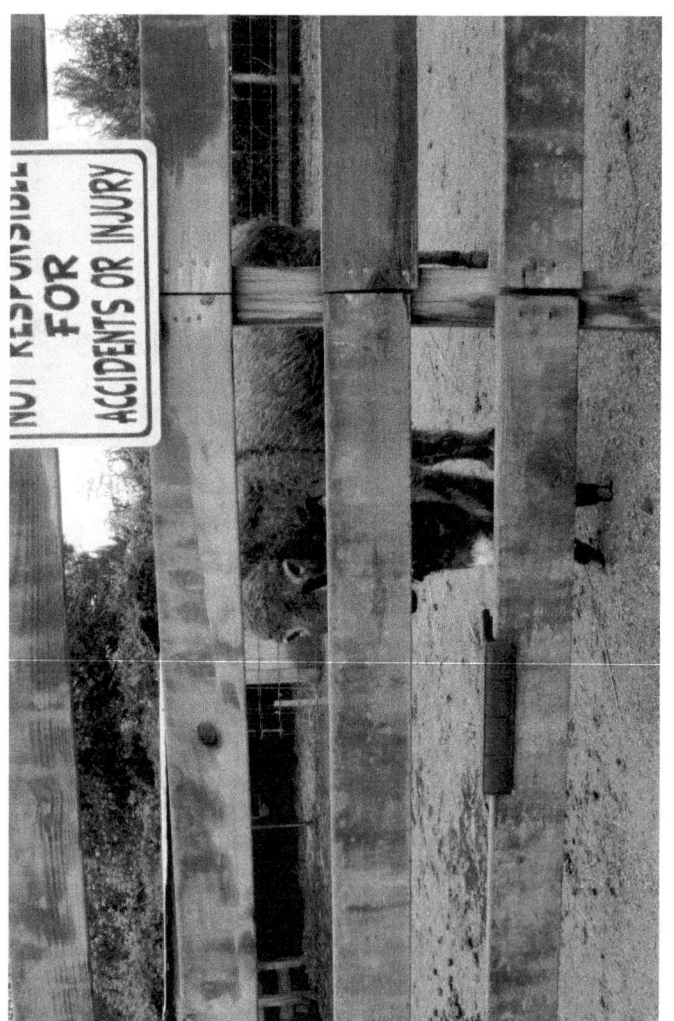

42

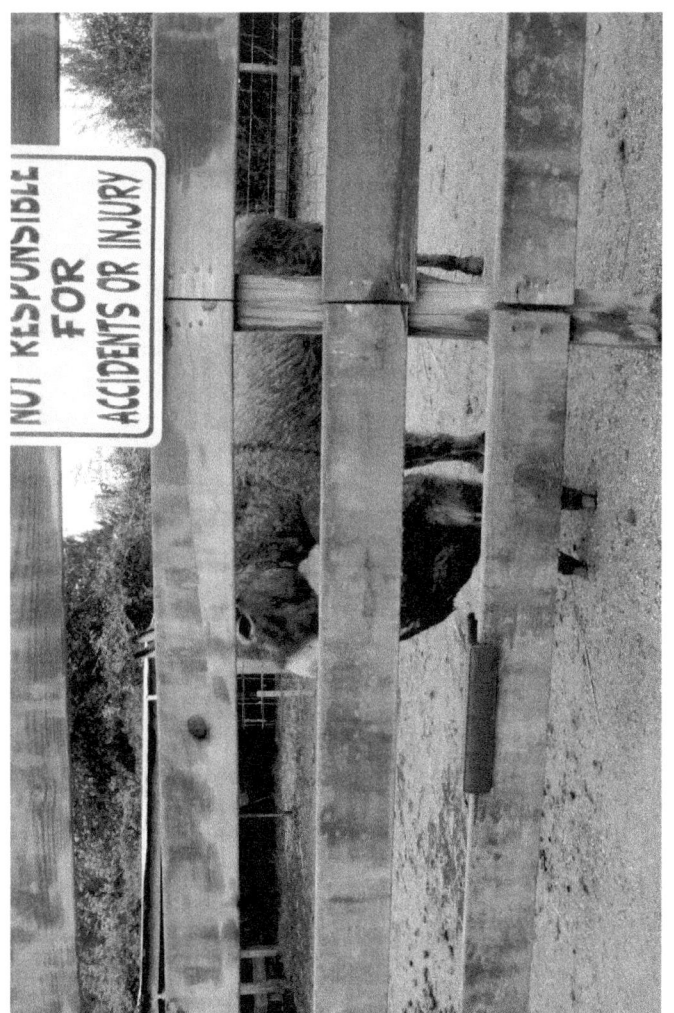

43

44

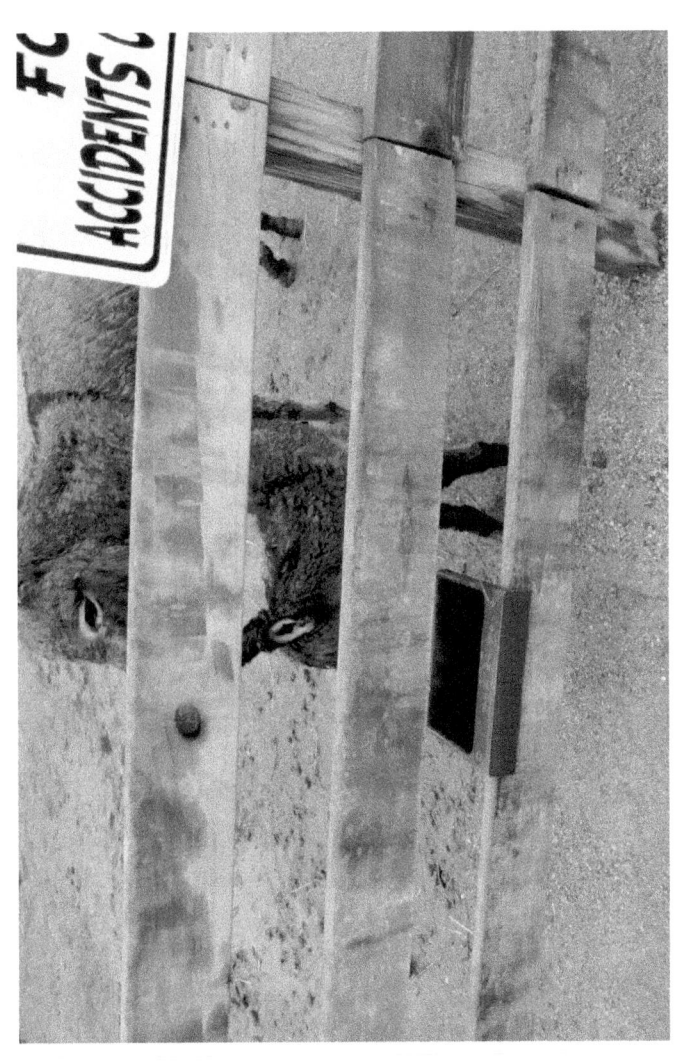

45

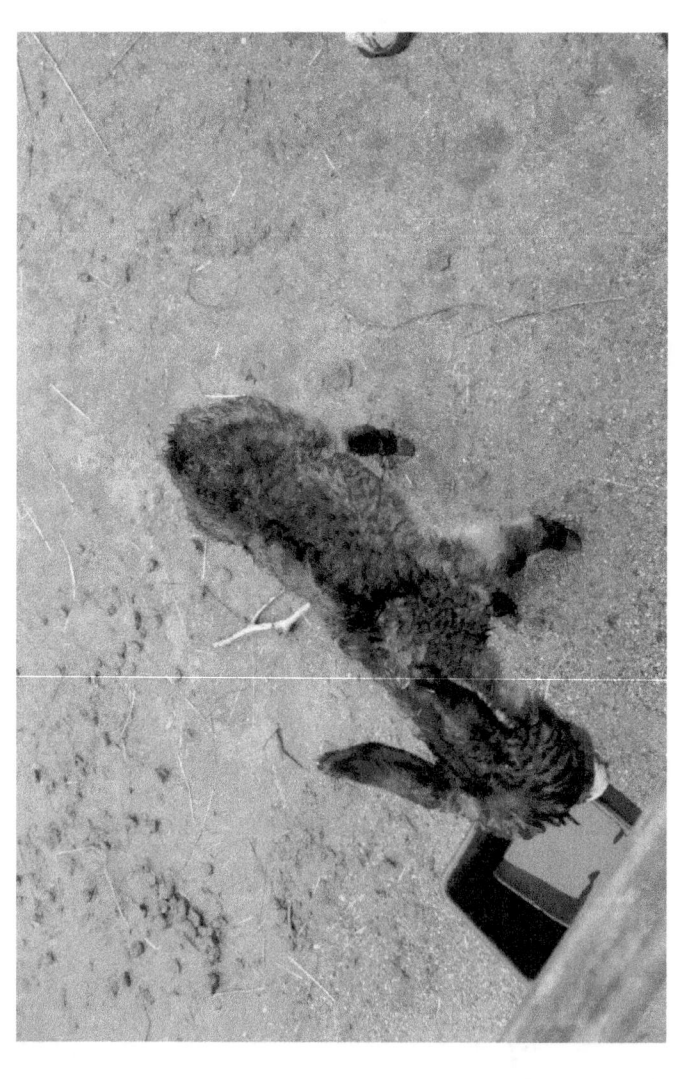

46

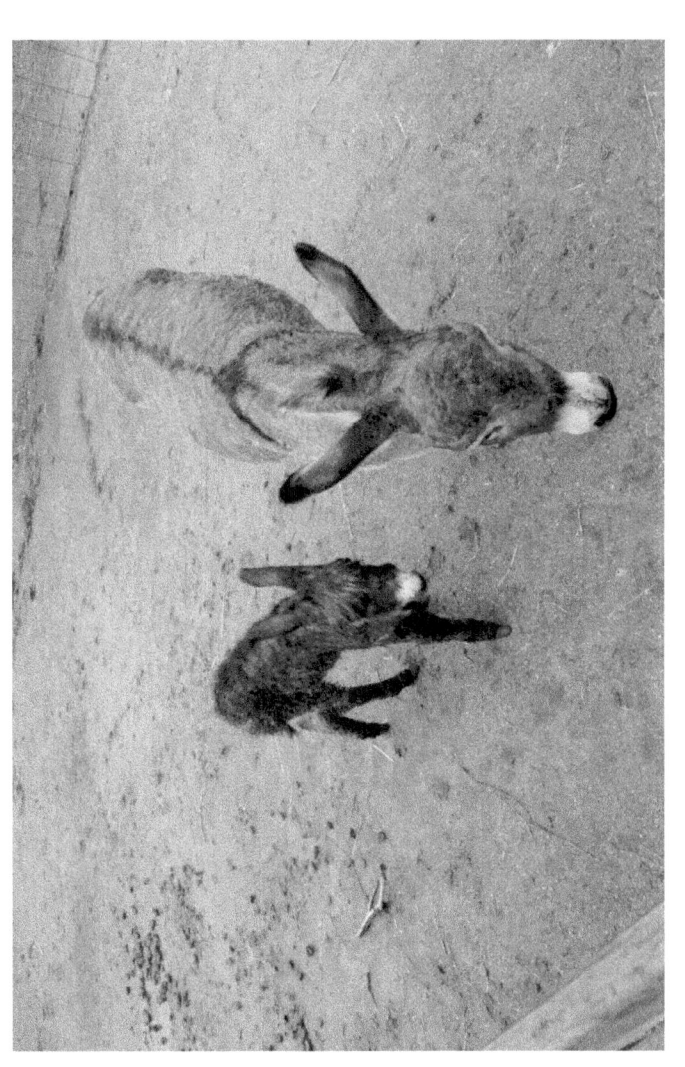

47

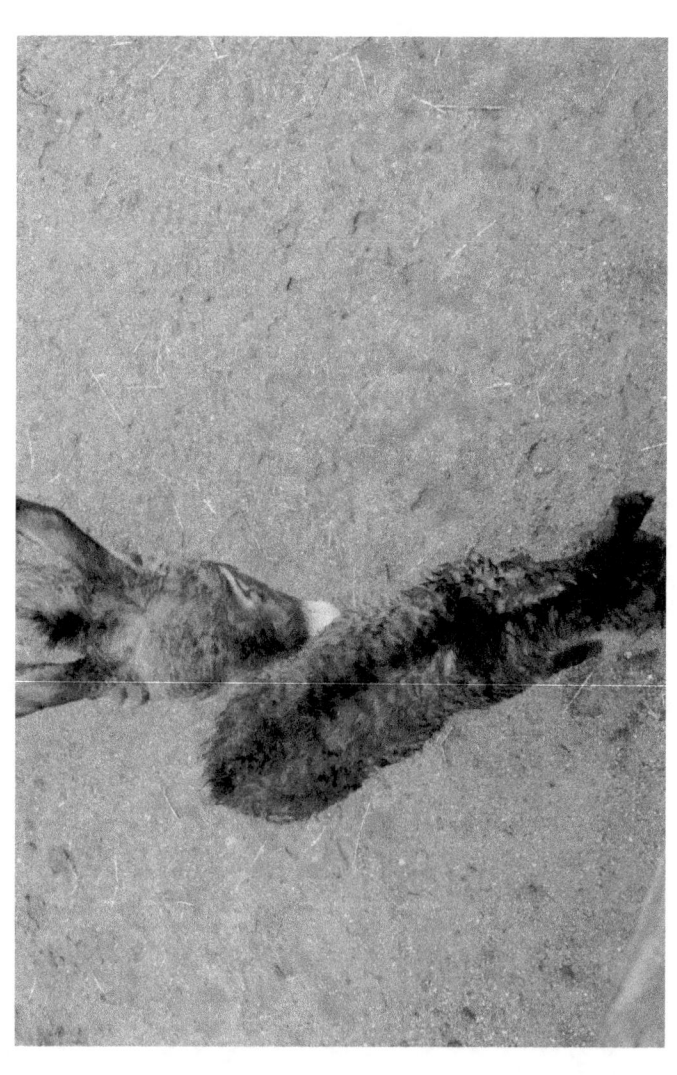

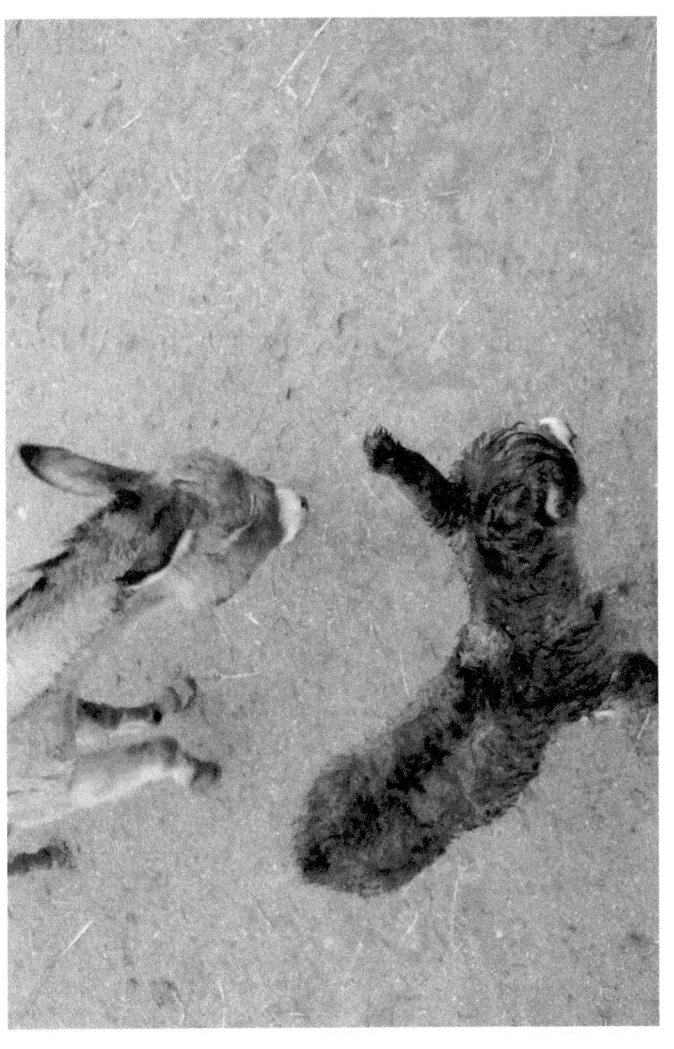

49

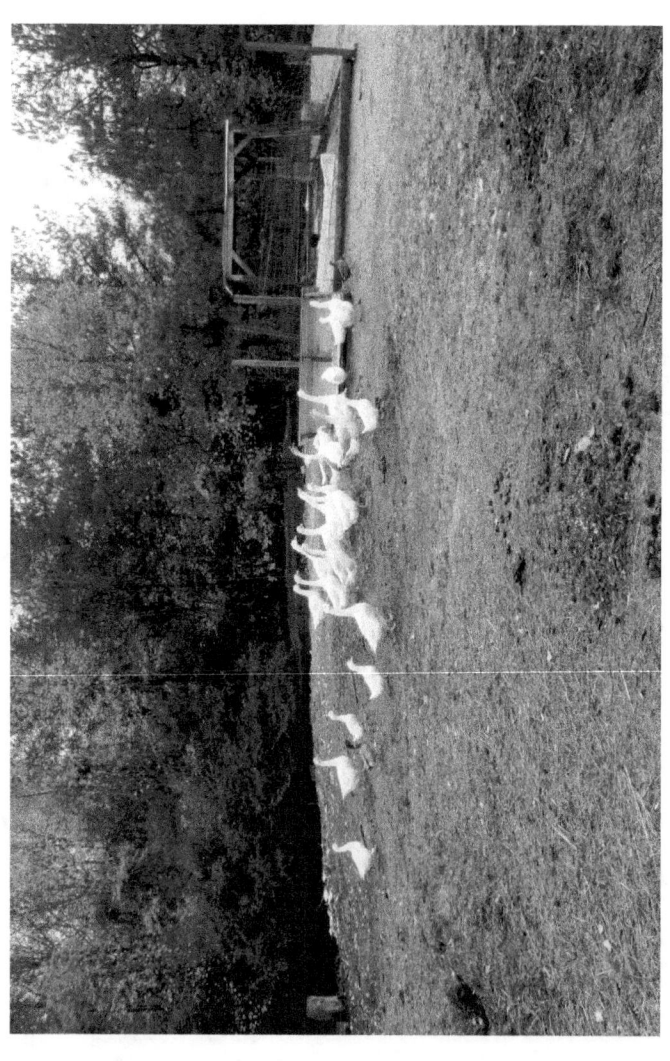

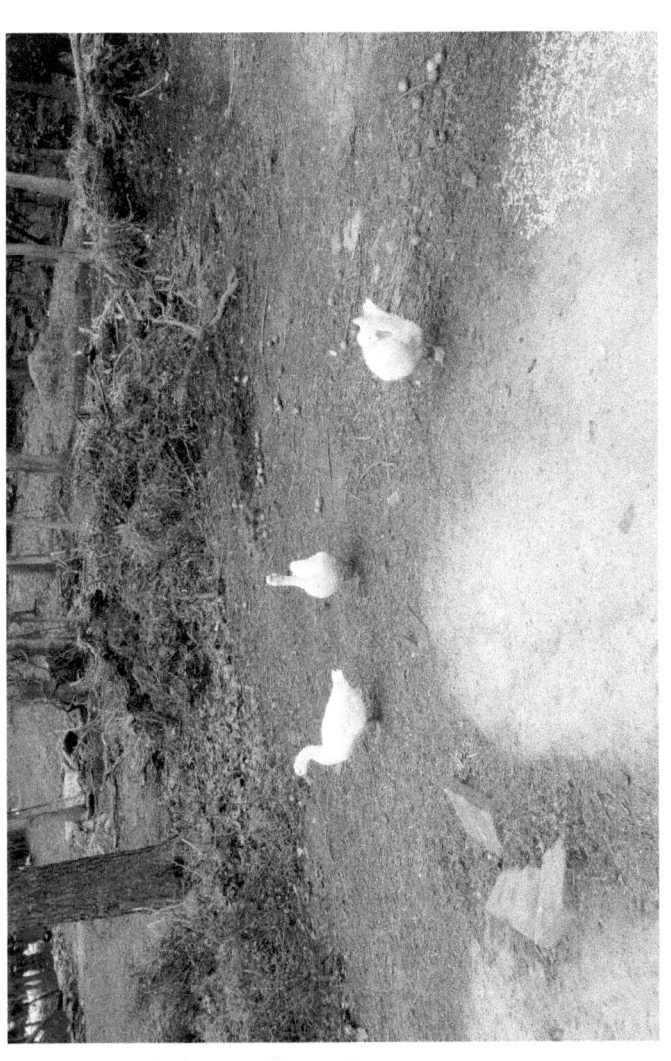

51

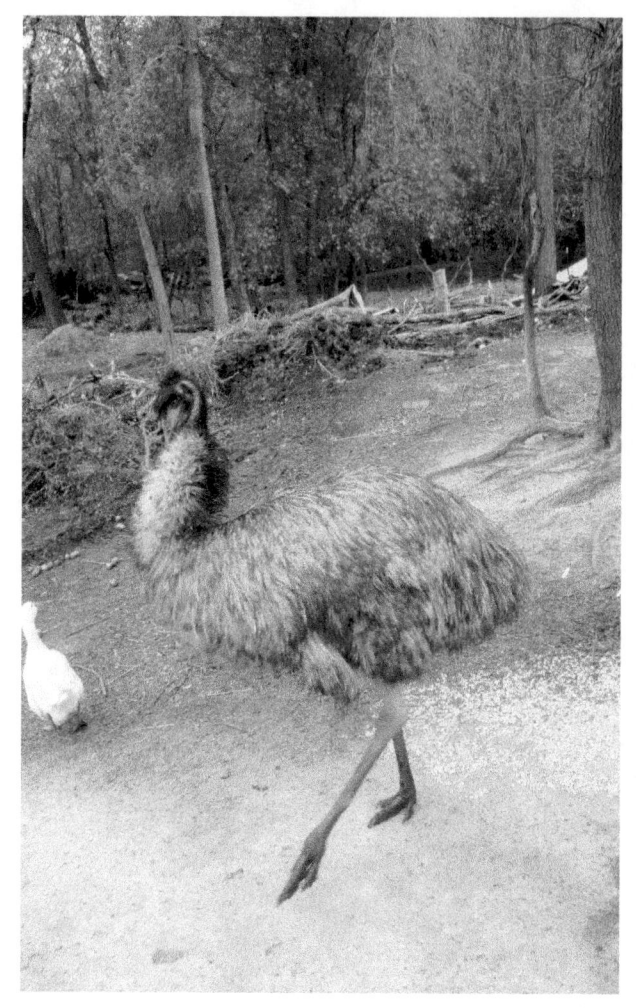

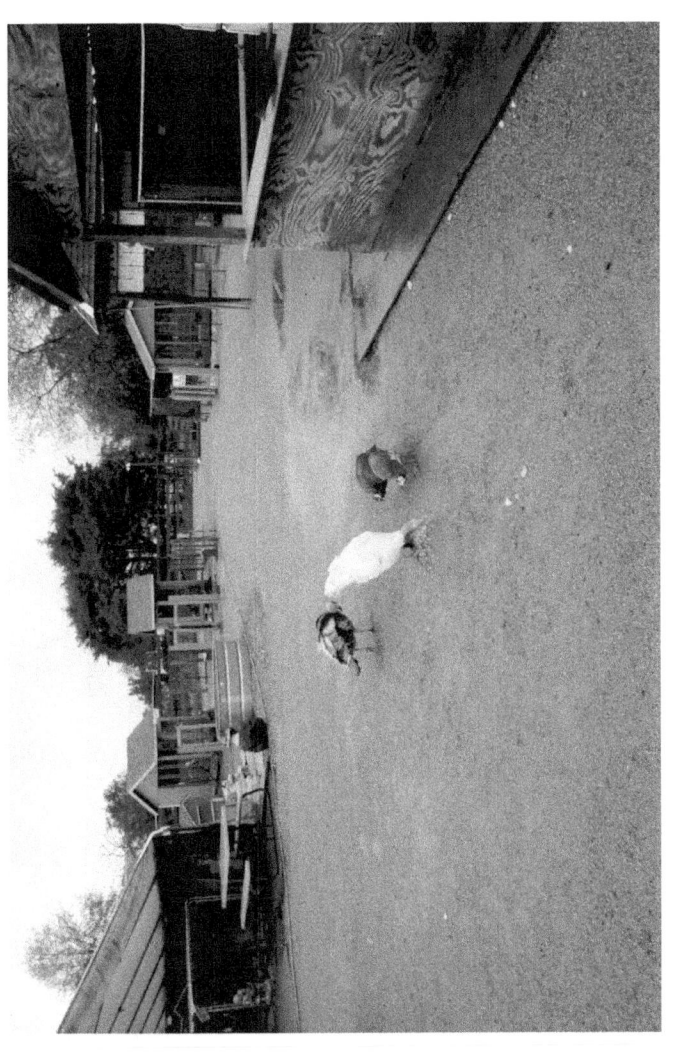

53

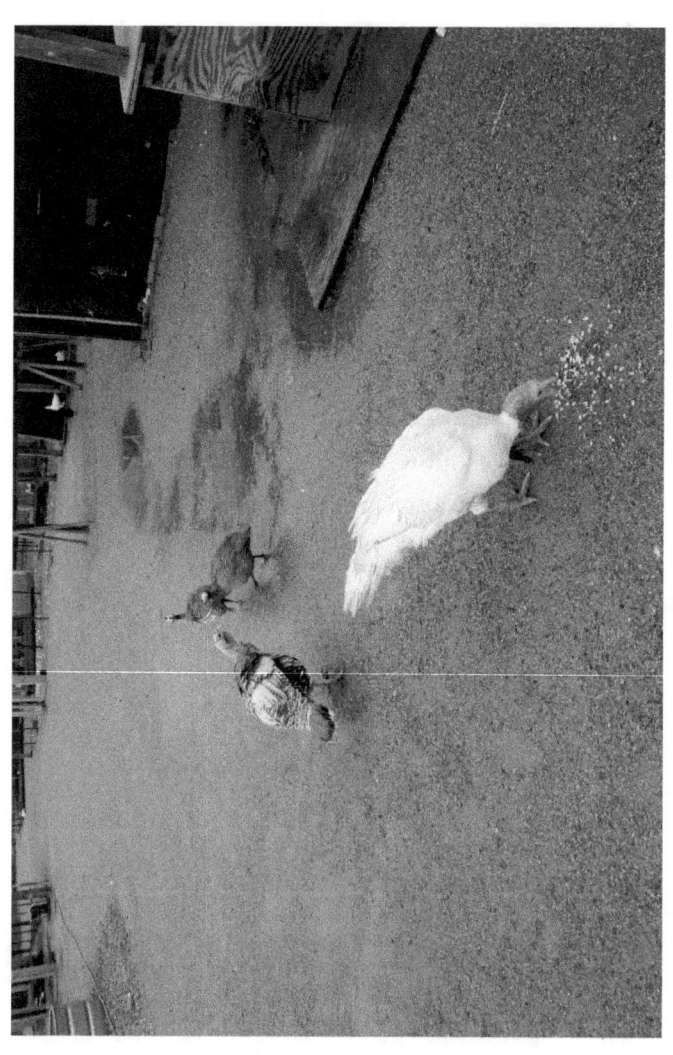

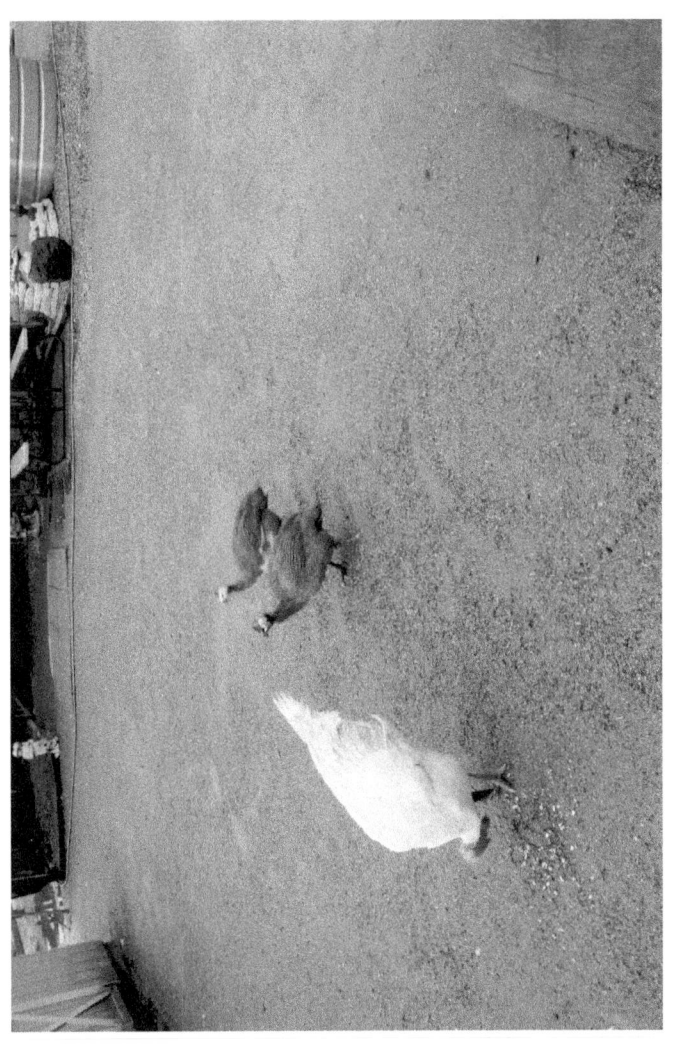

55

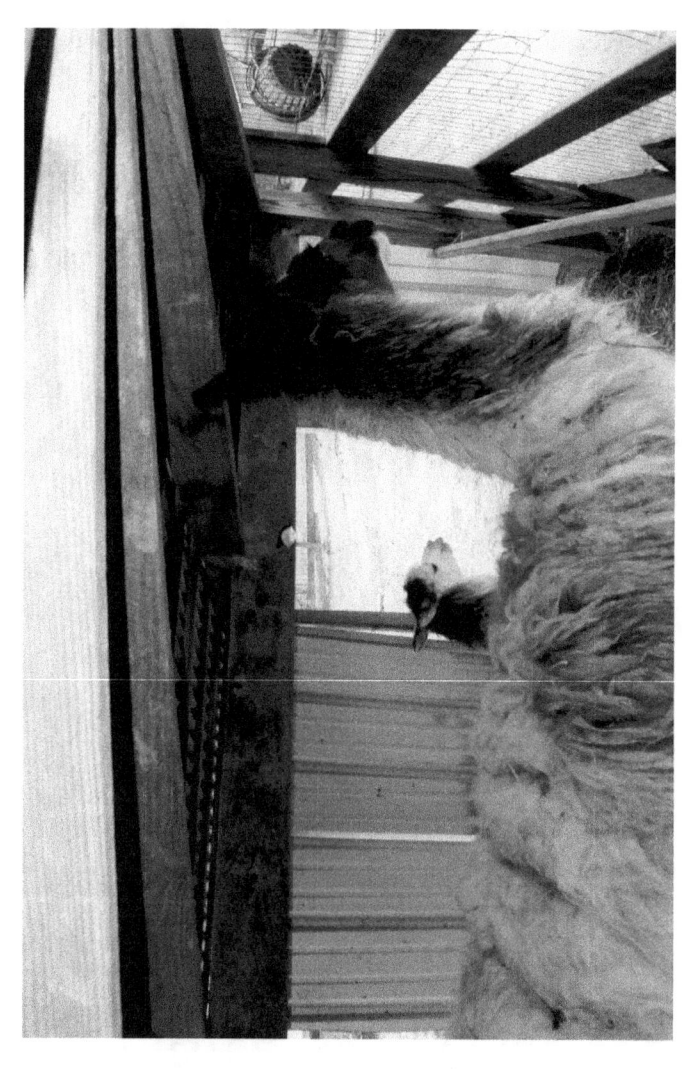

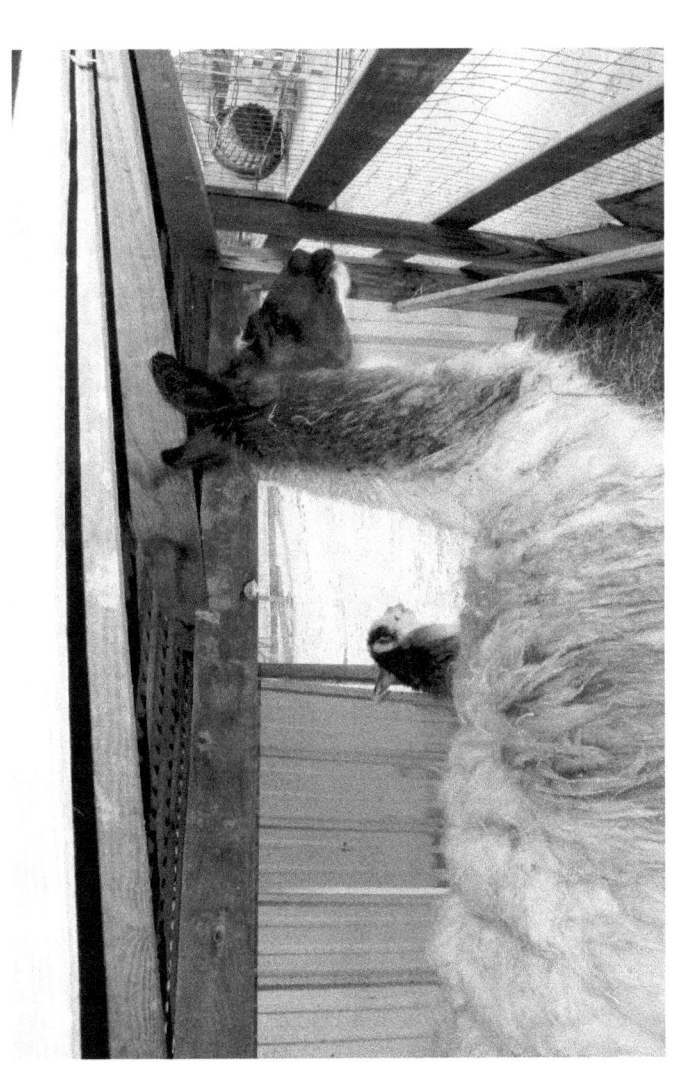

57

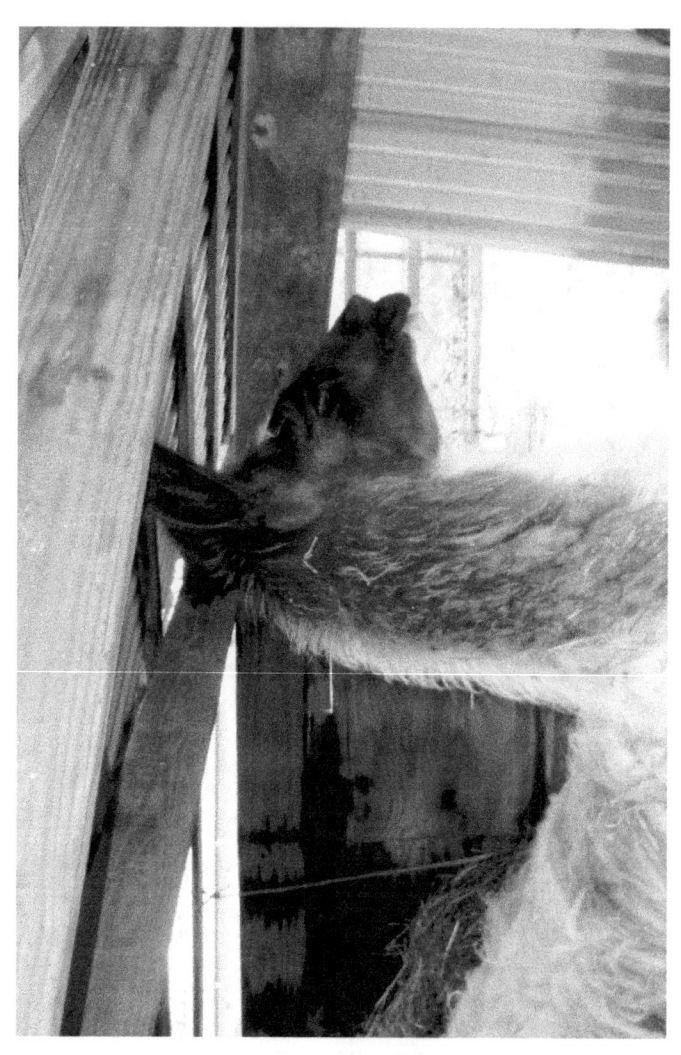

58

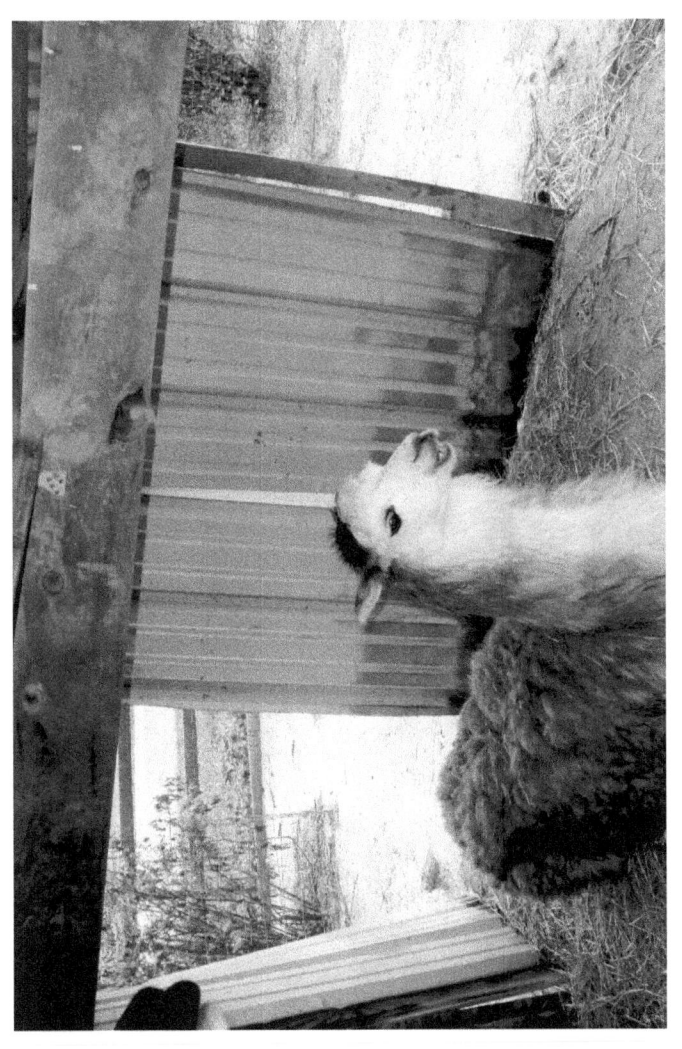

59

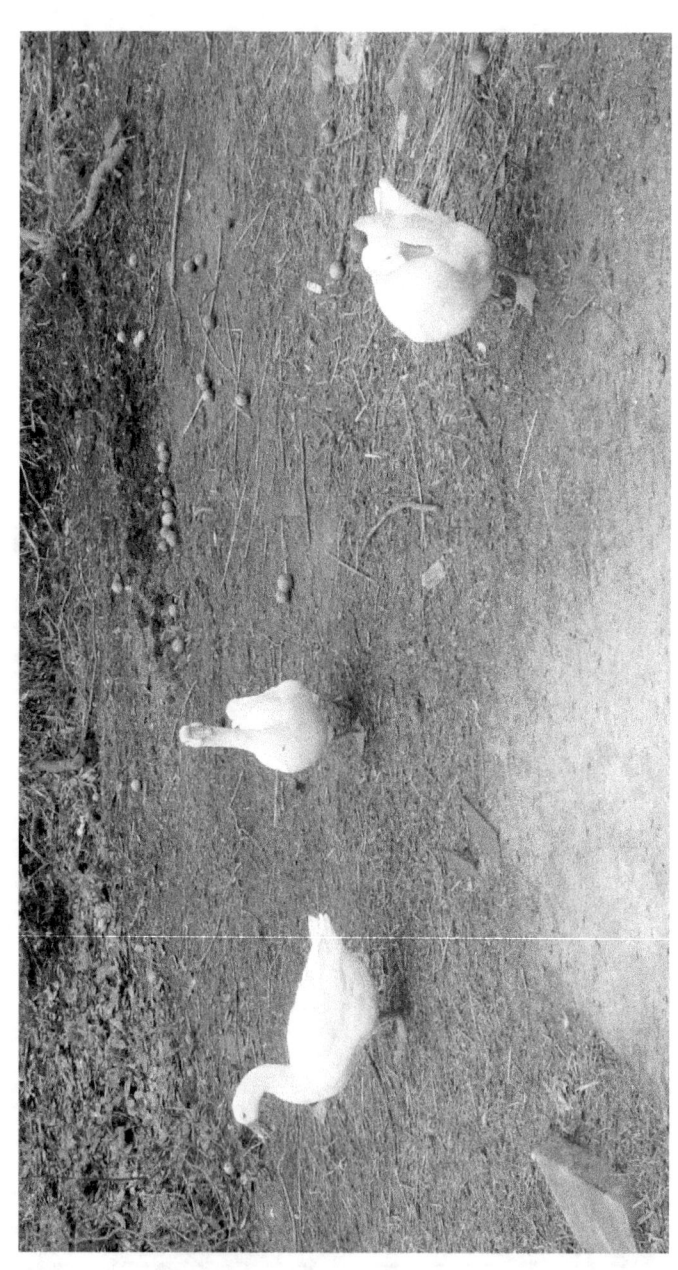

60

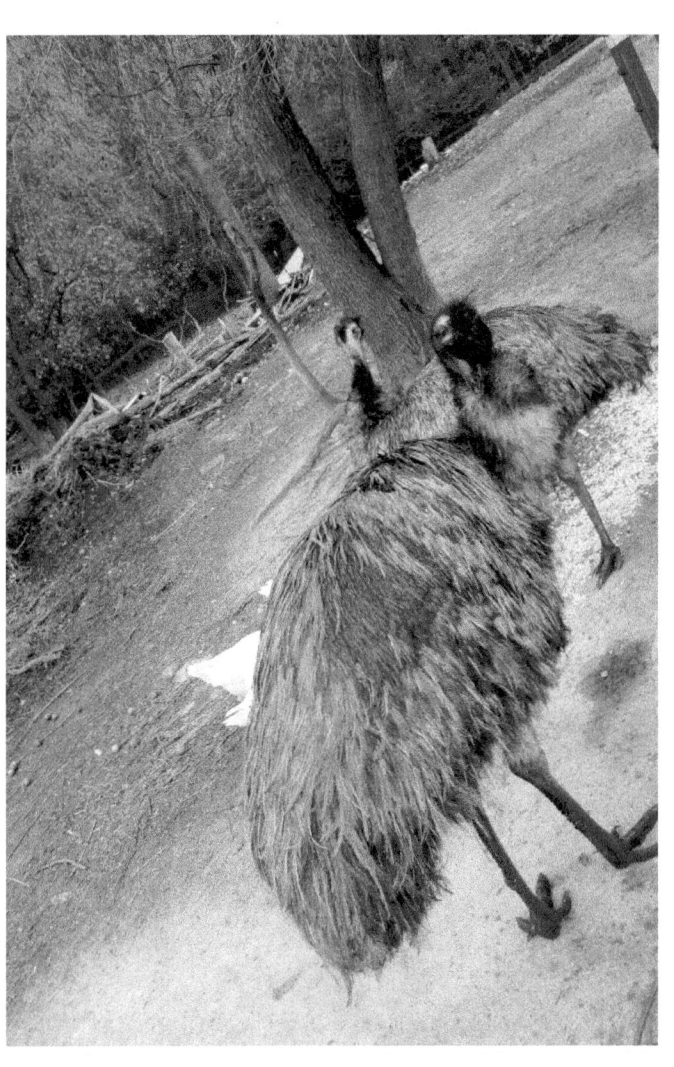

61

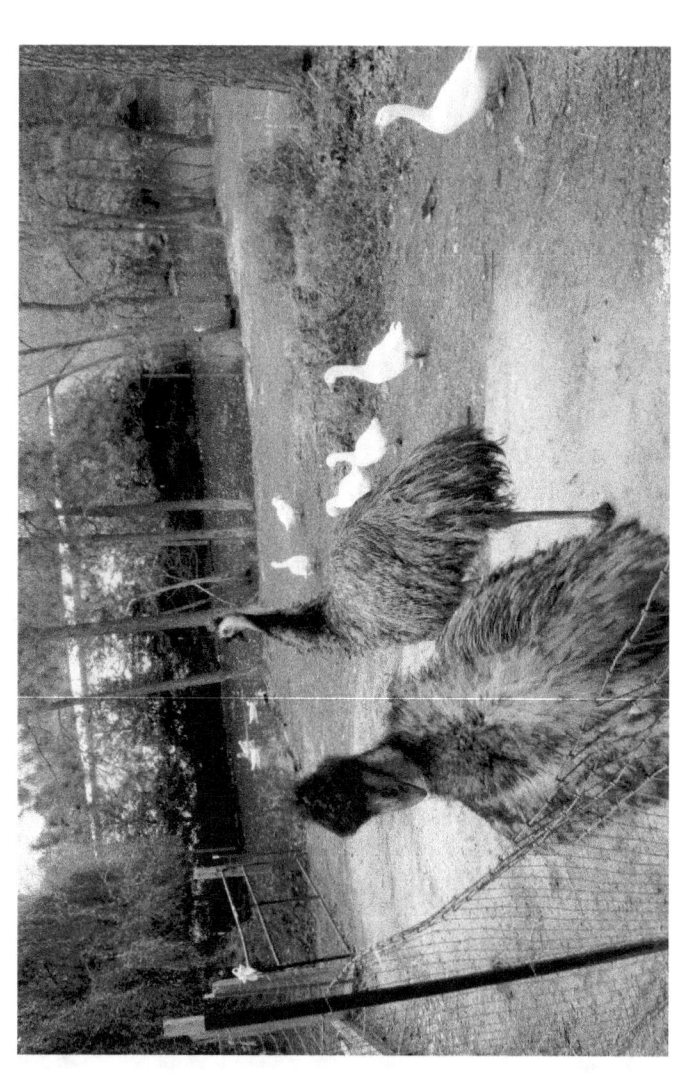

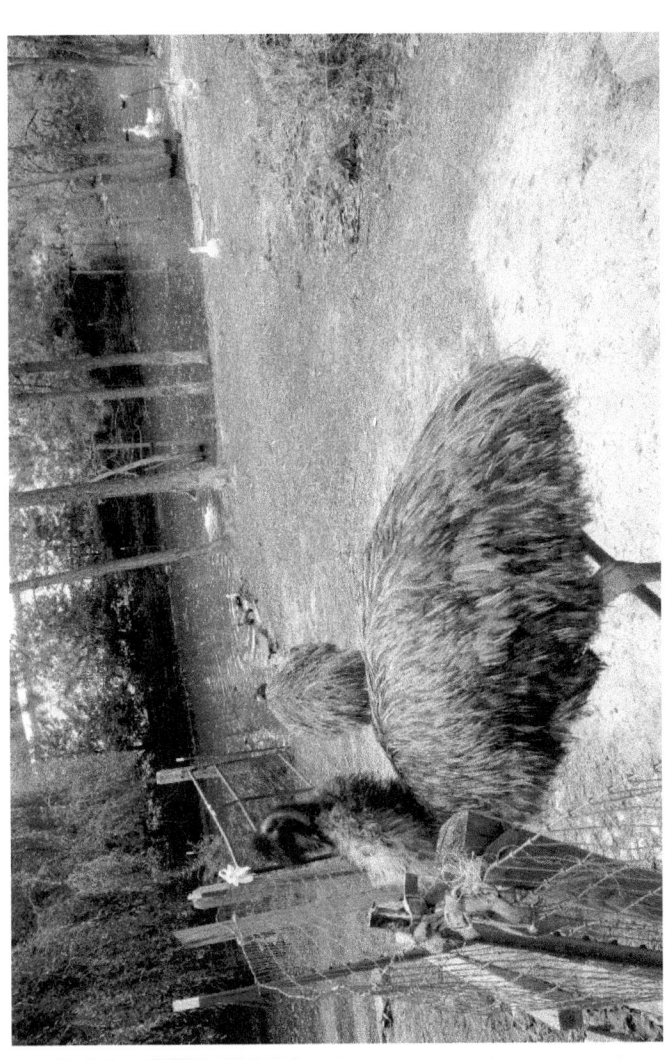

63

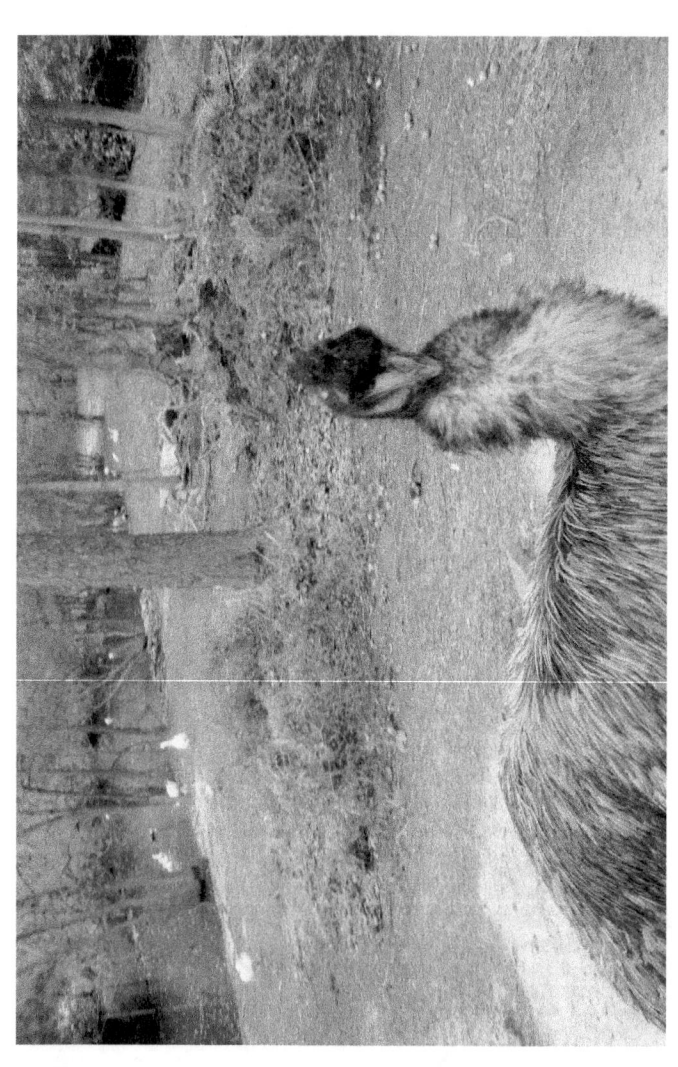

64

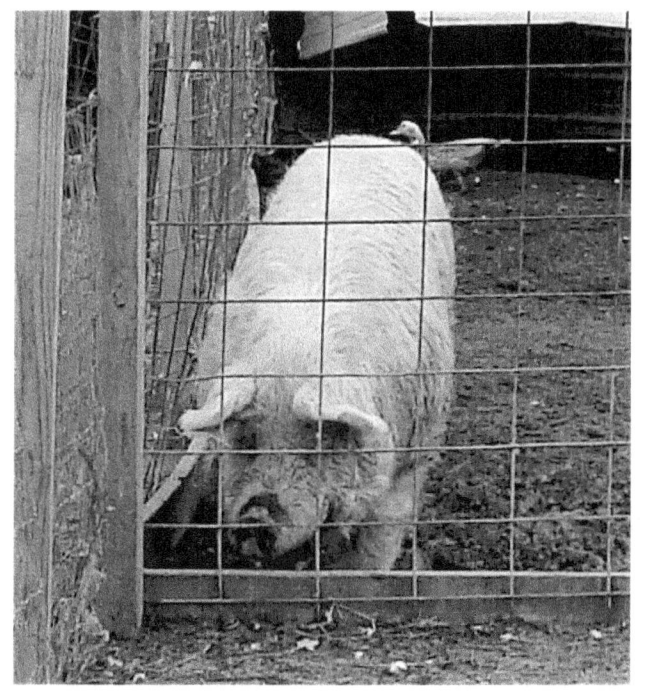

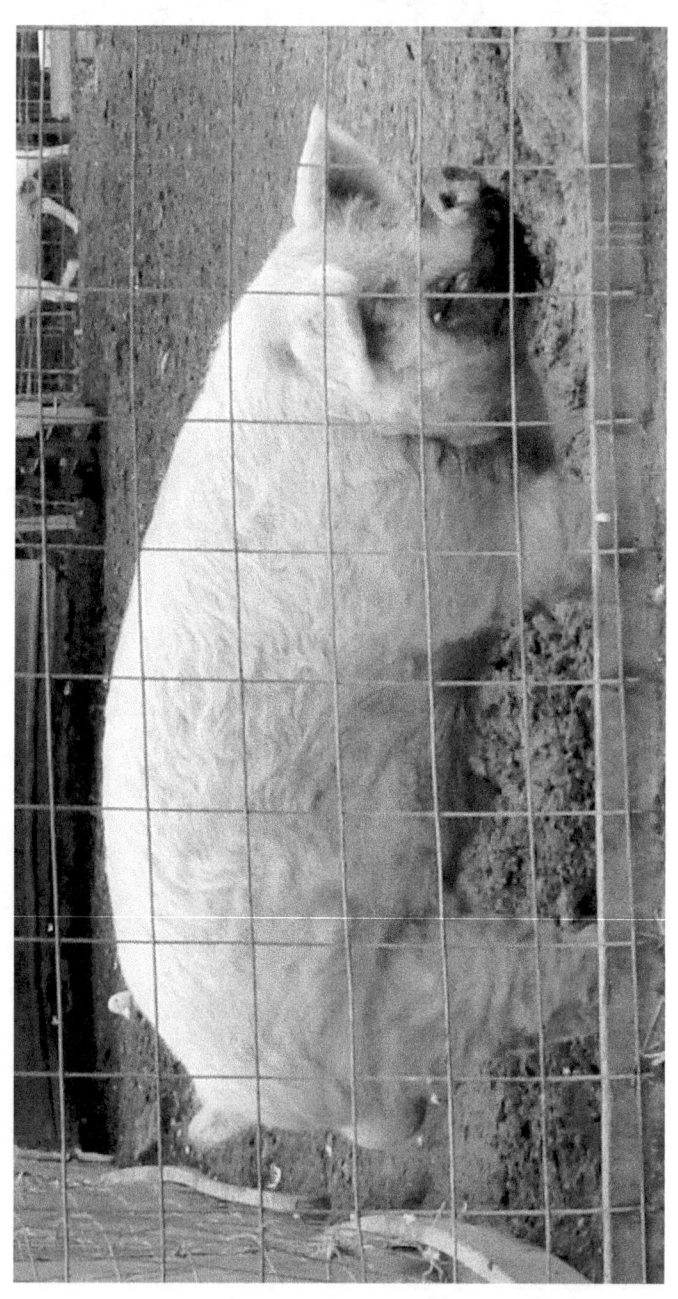

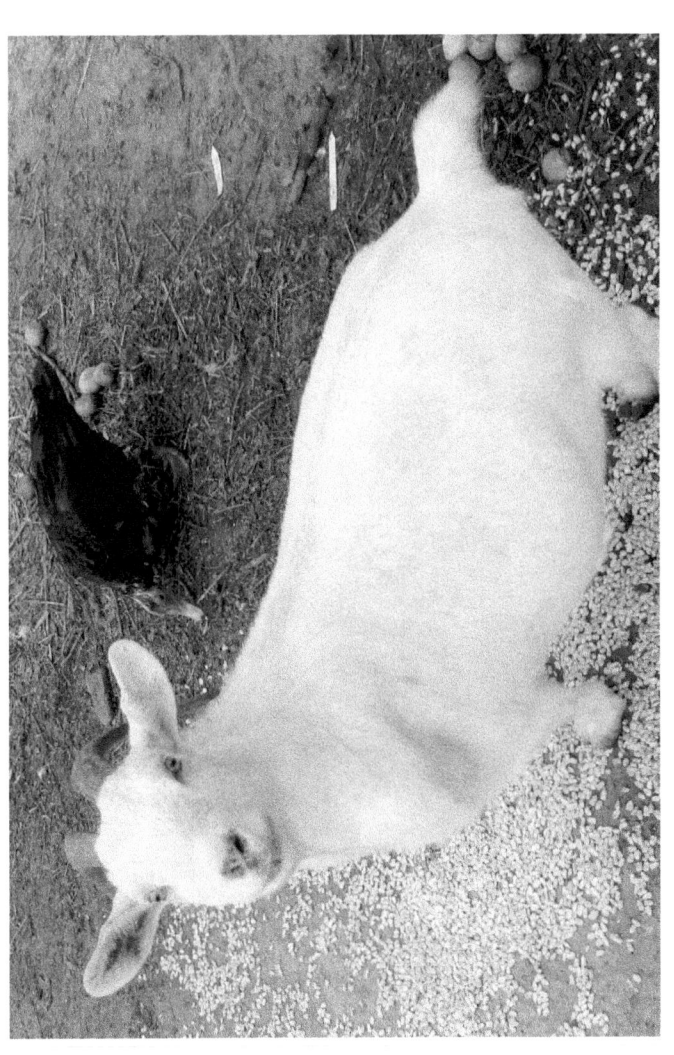

67

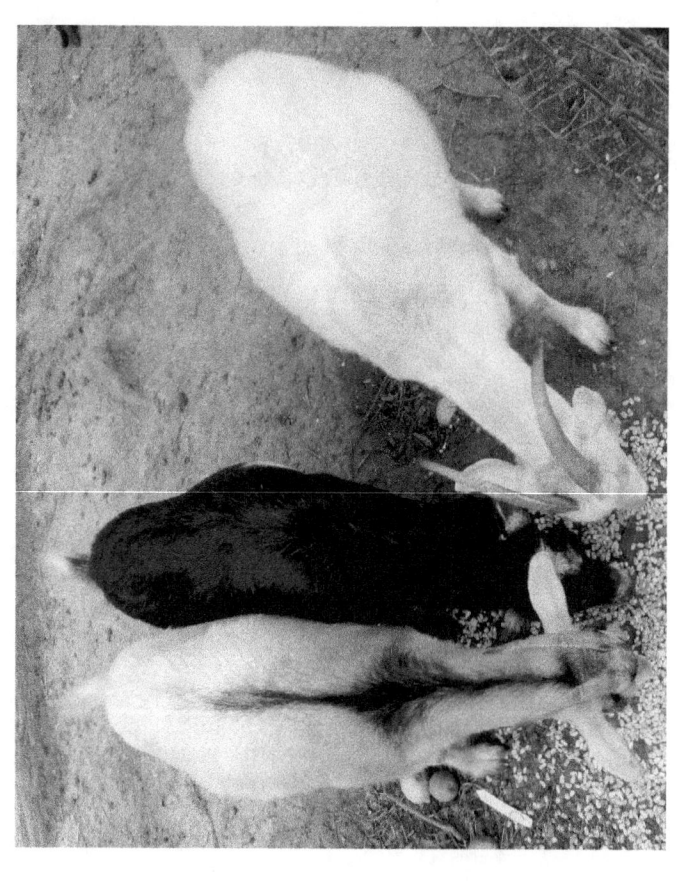

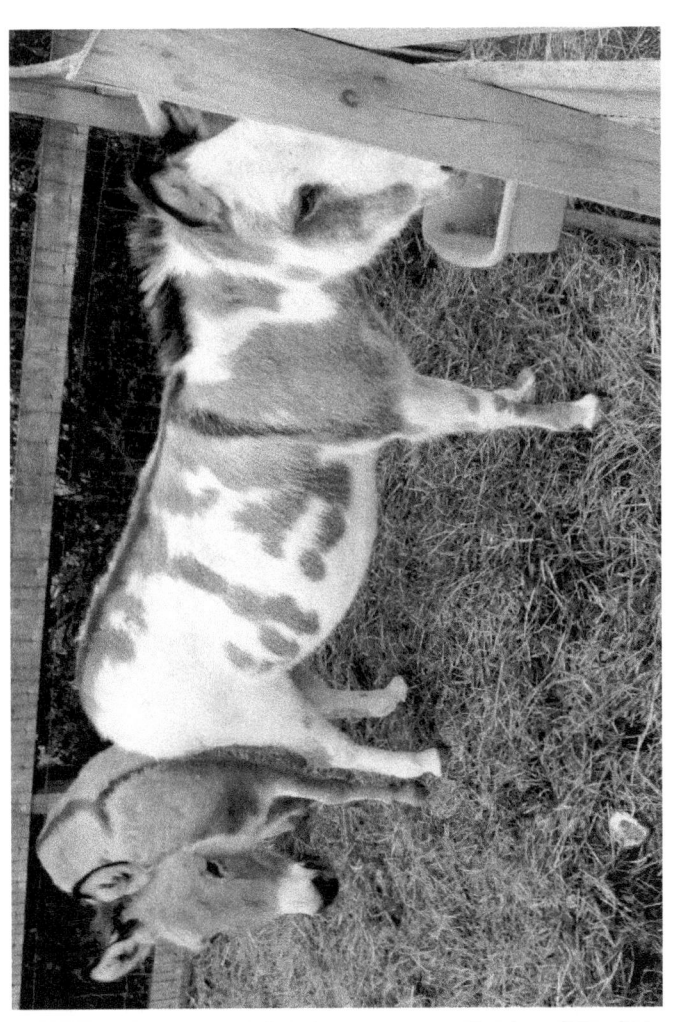

69

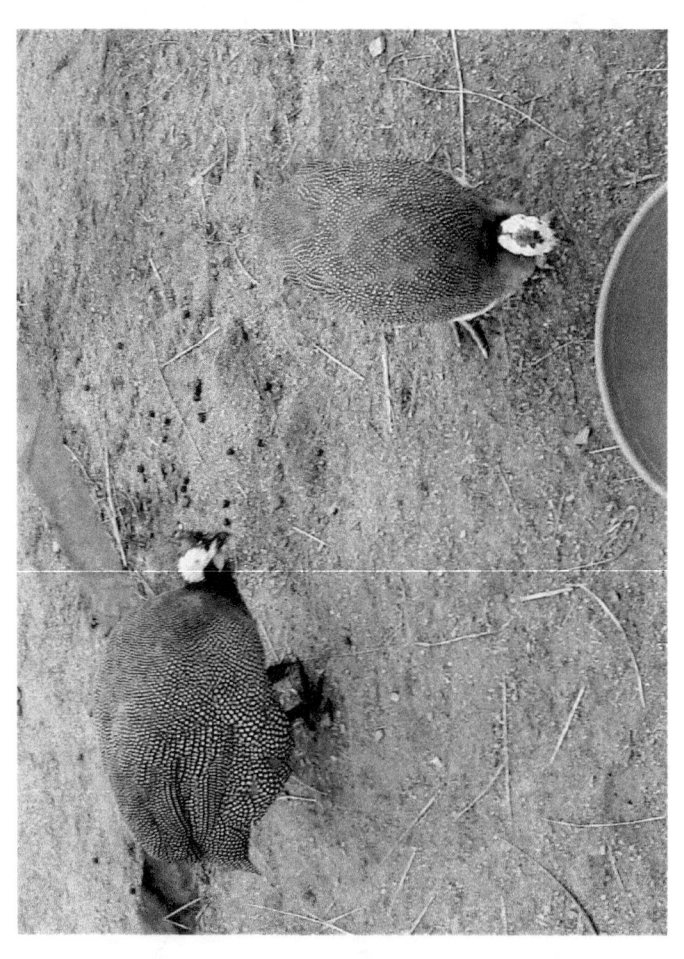

70

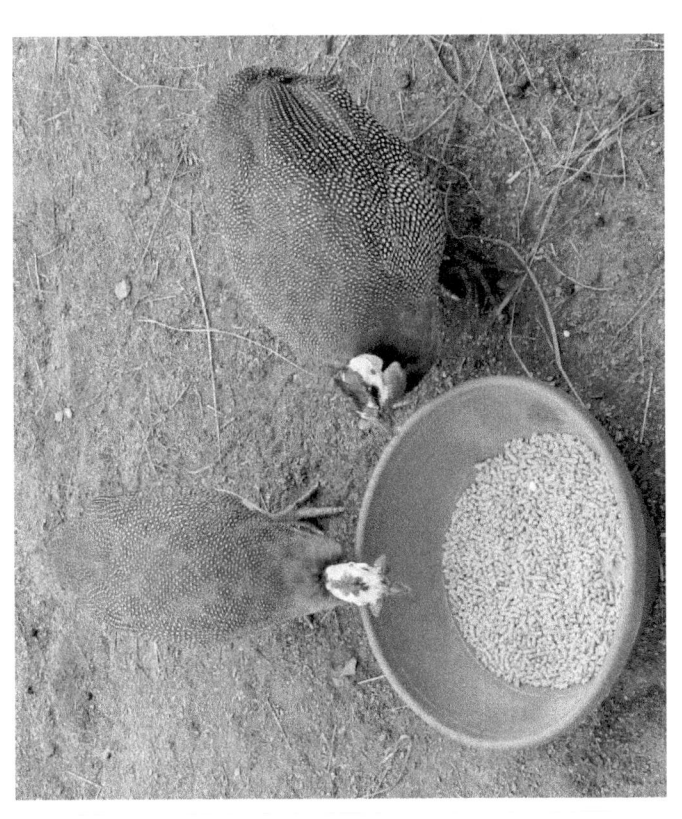

71

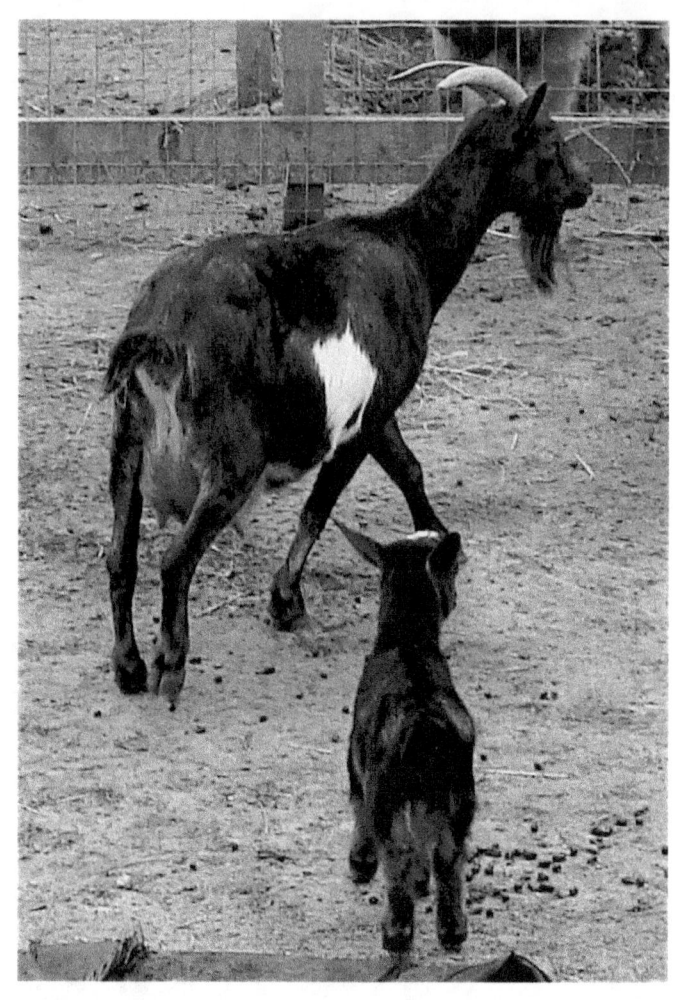

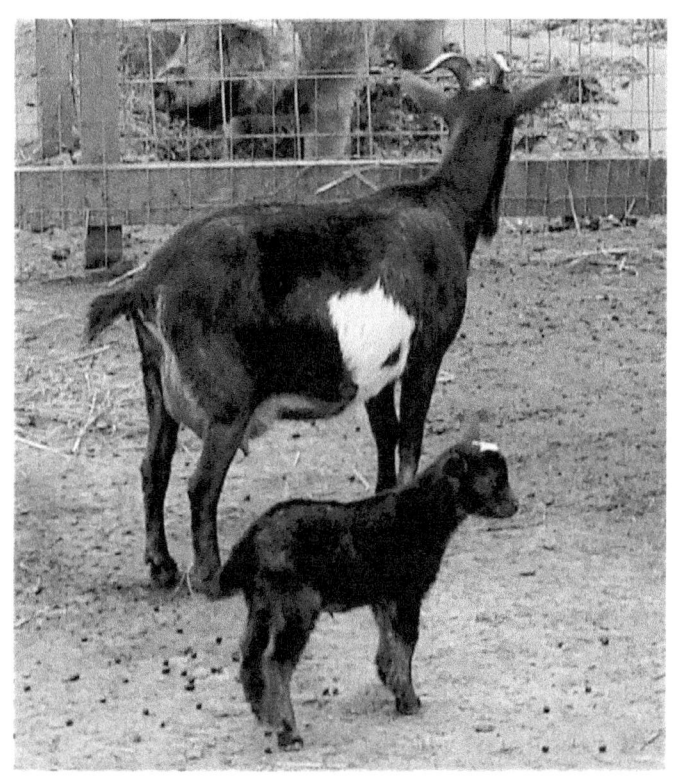

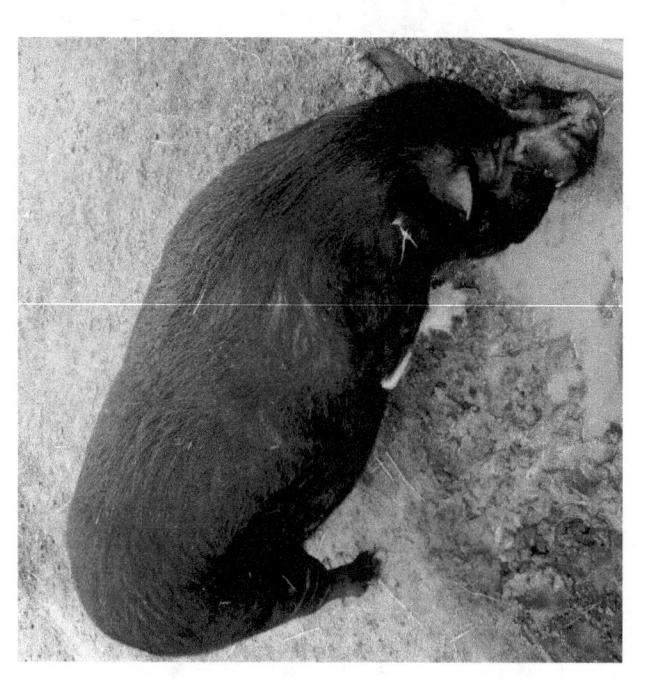

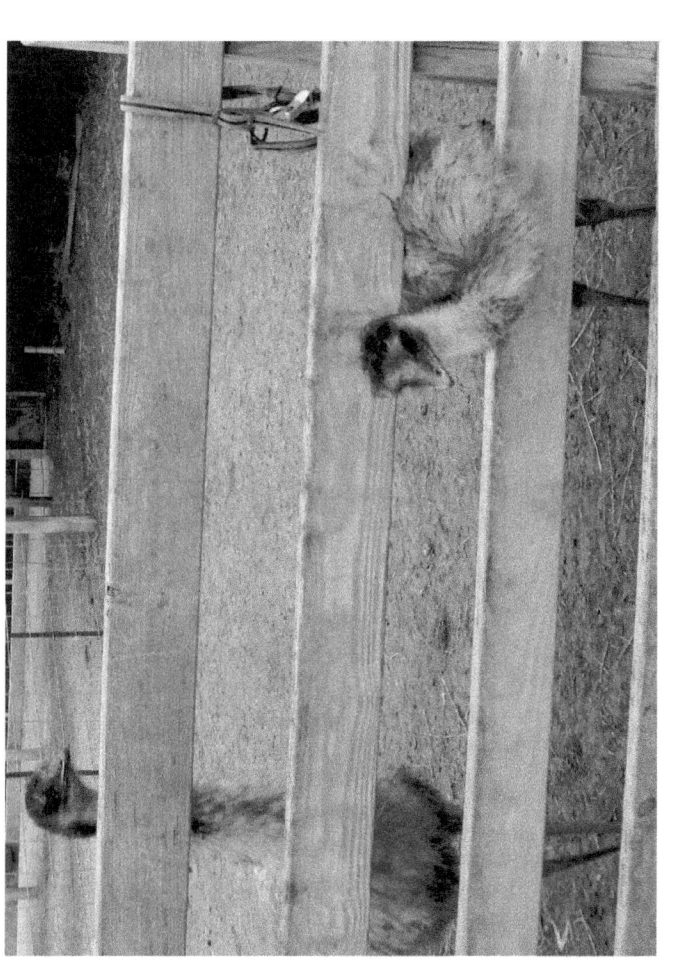

75

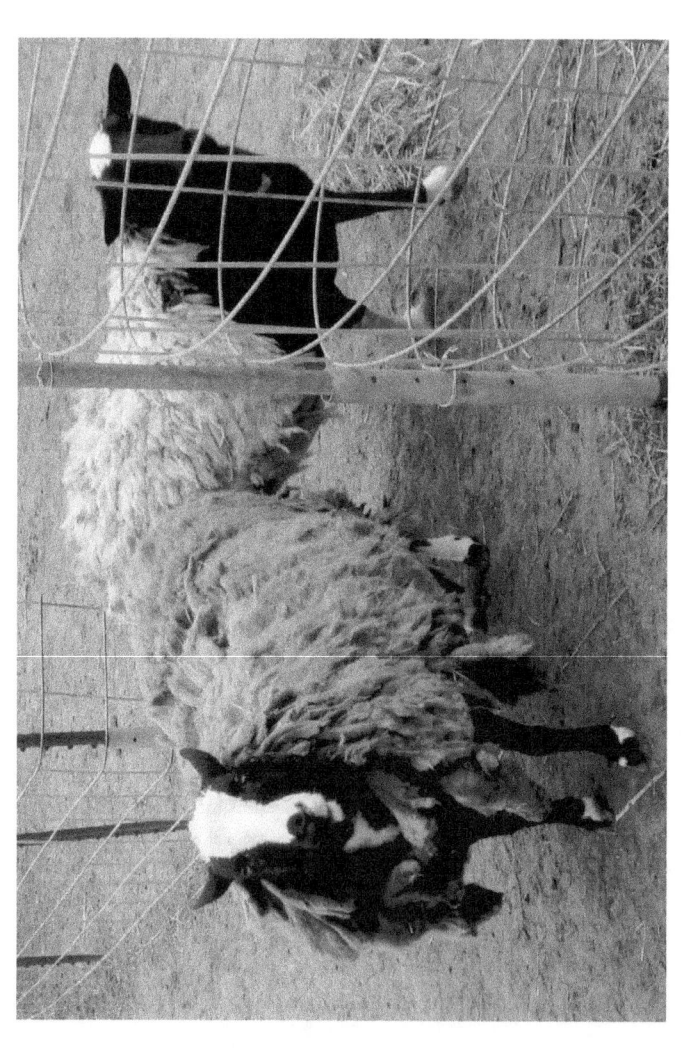

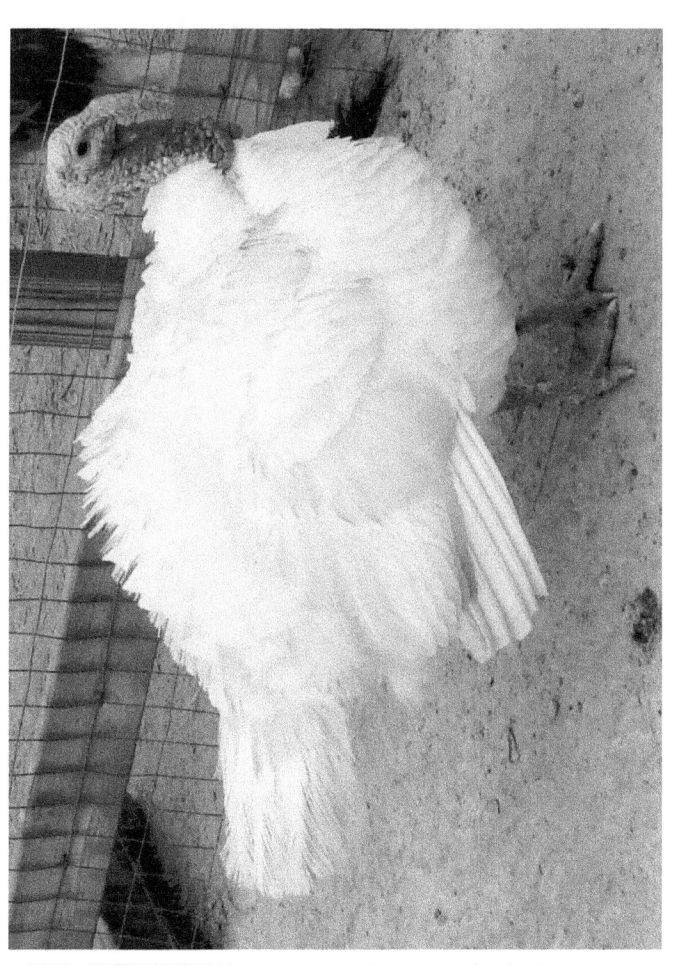

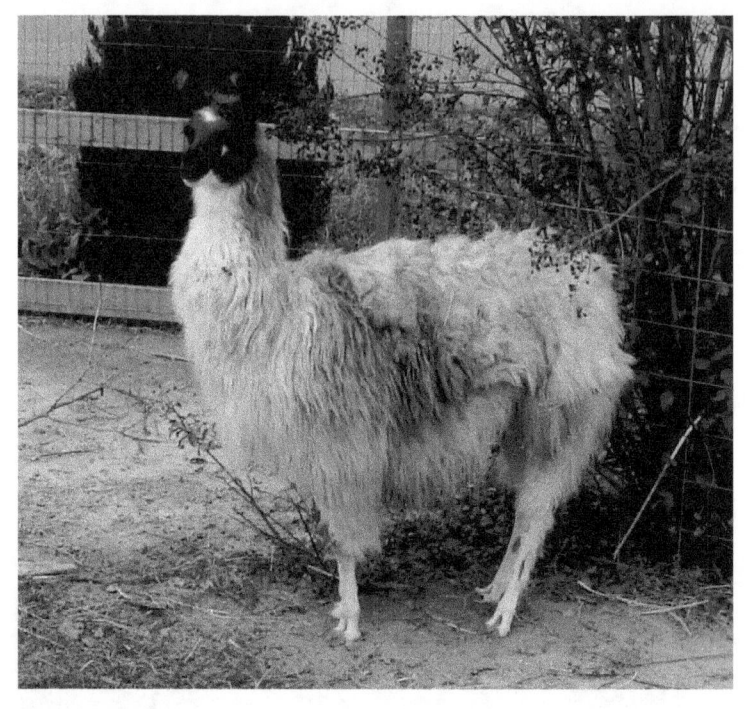

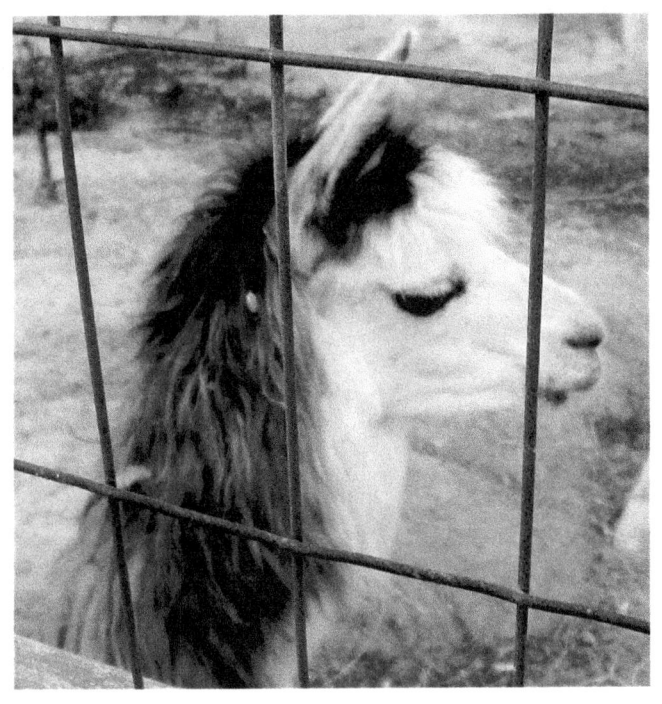

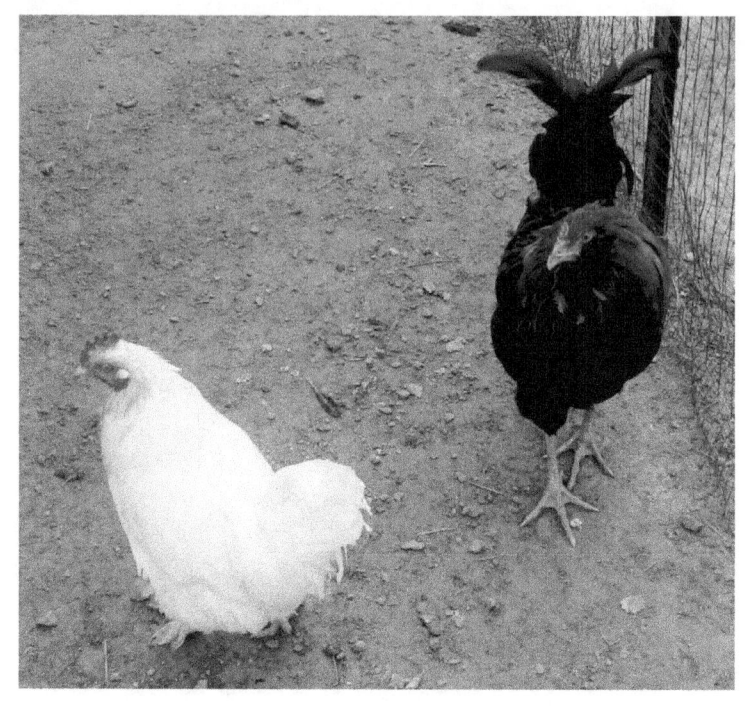

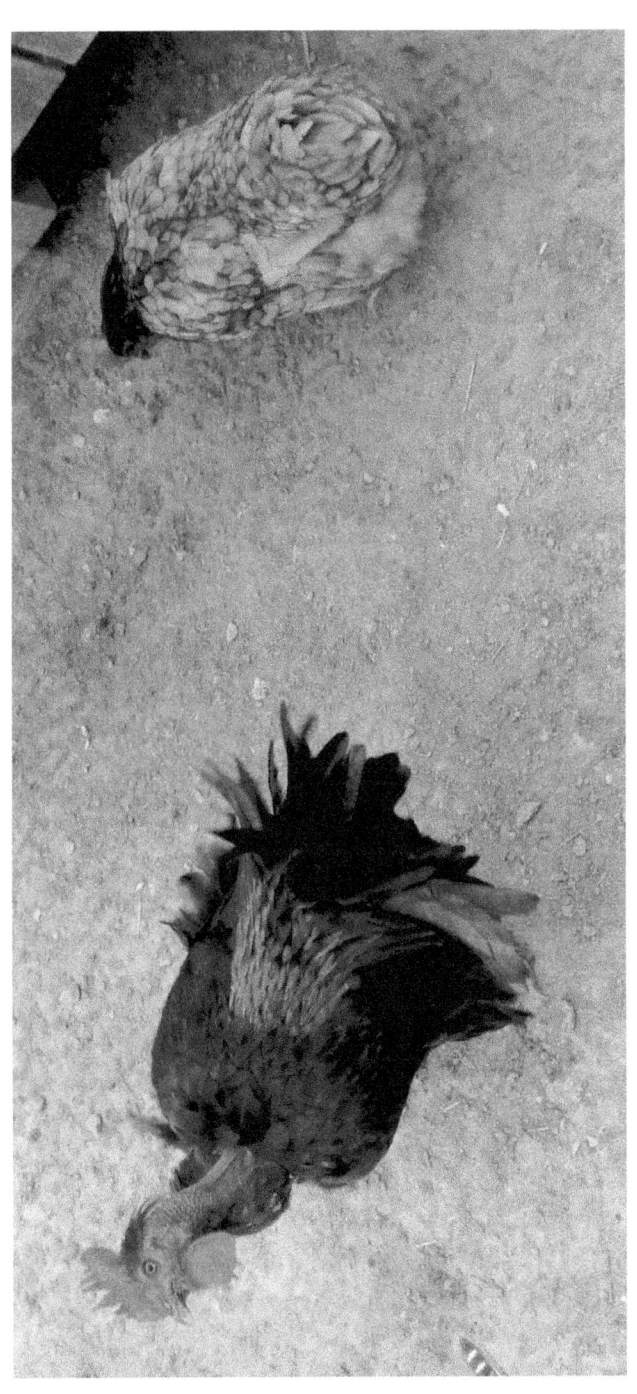

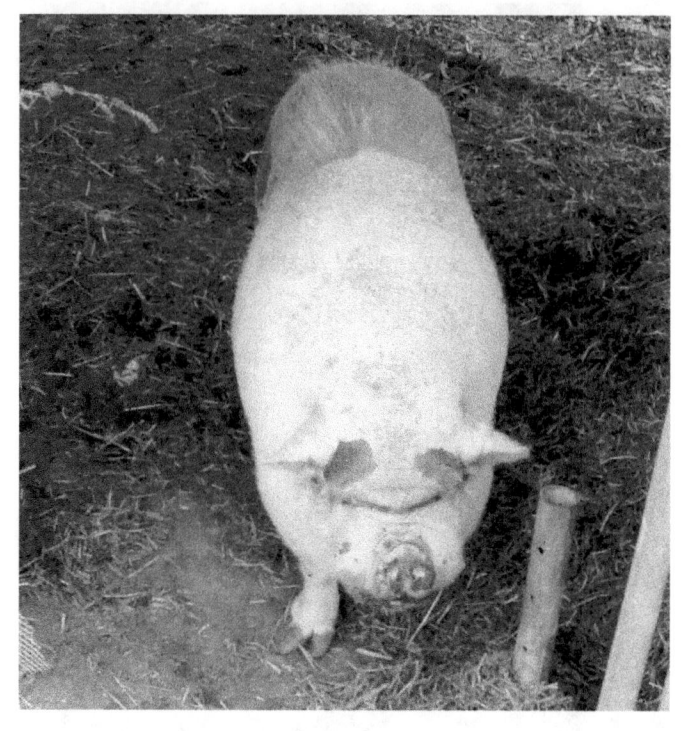

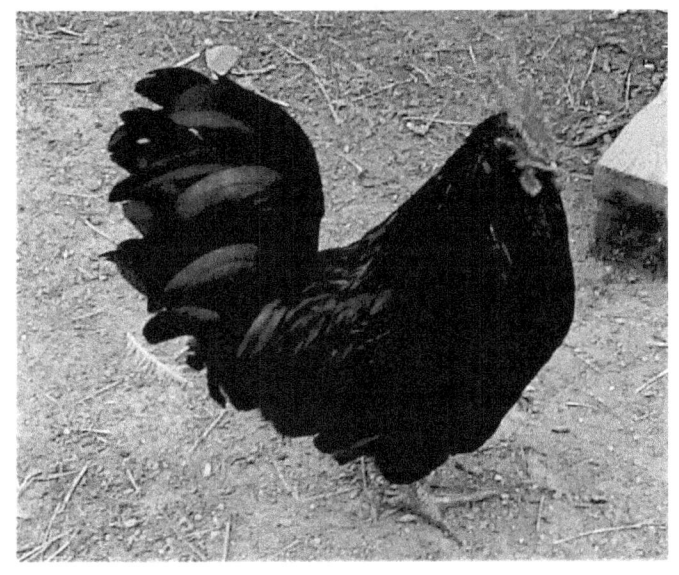

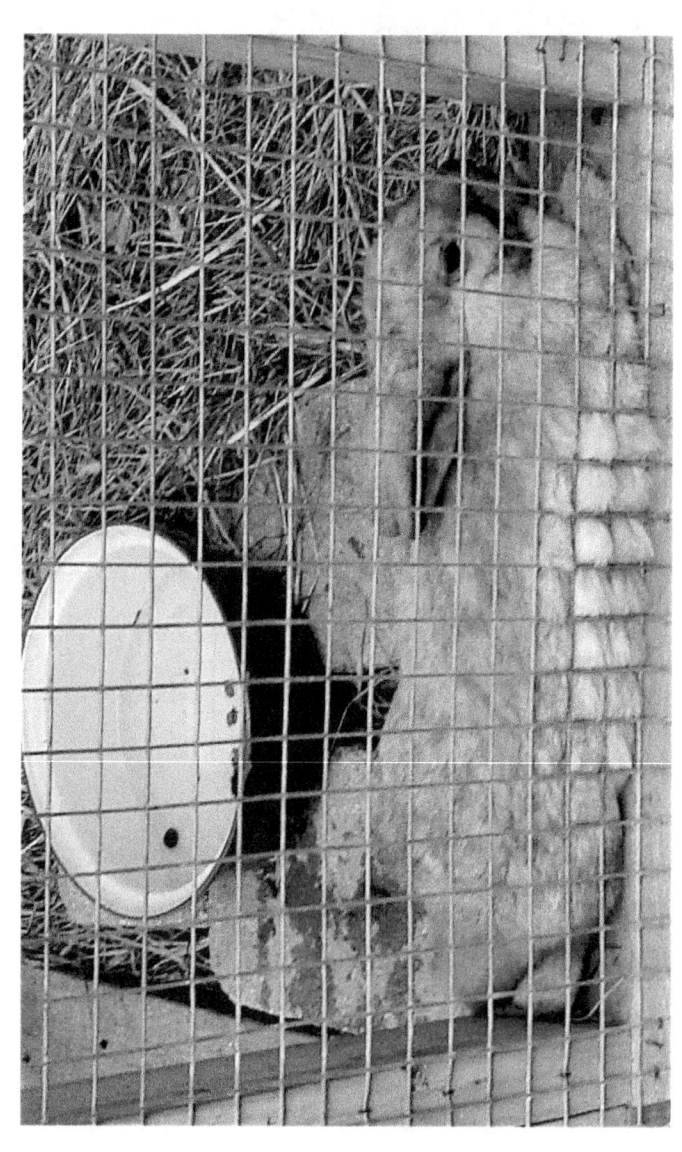

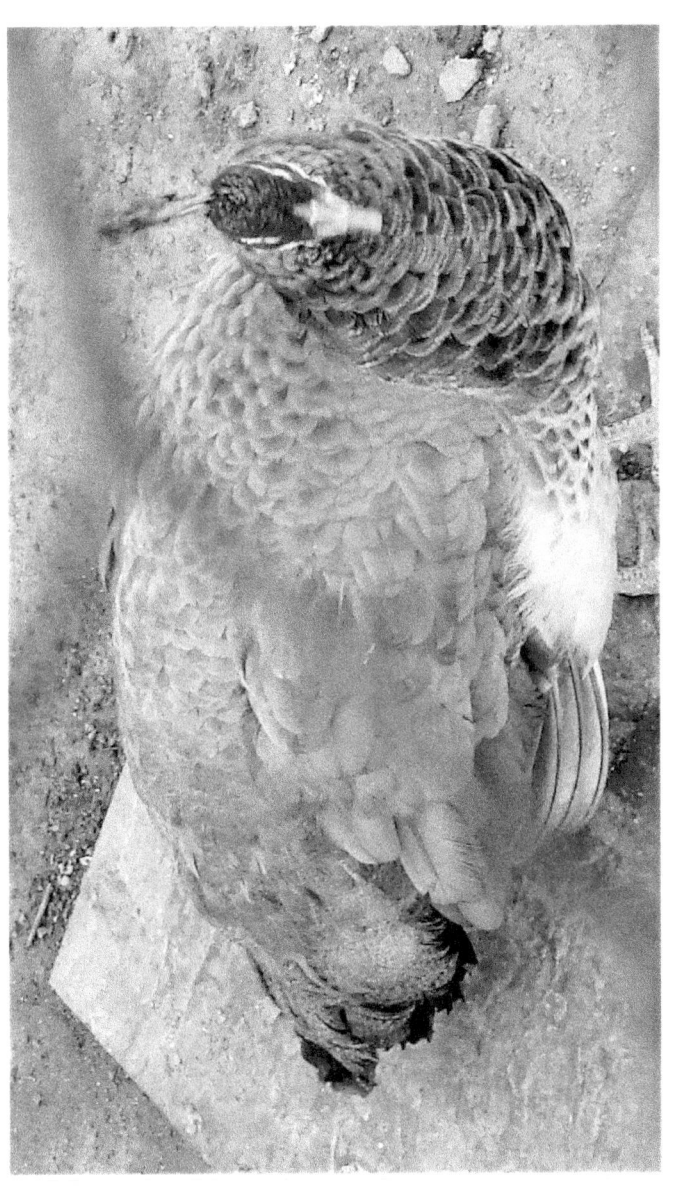

85

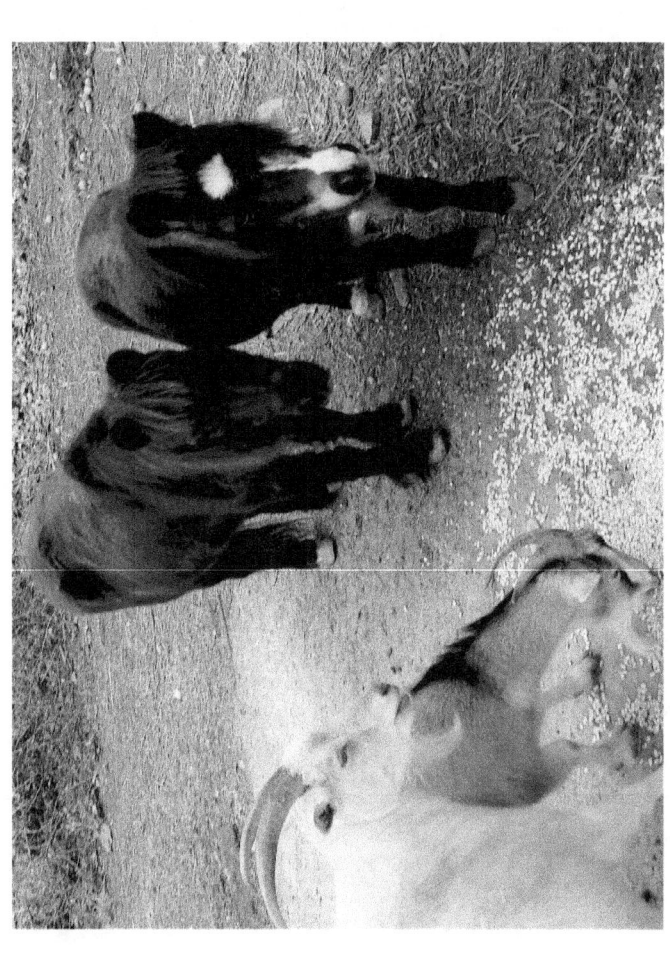

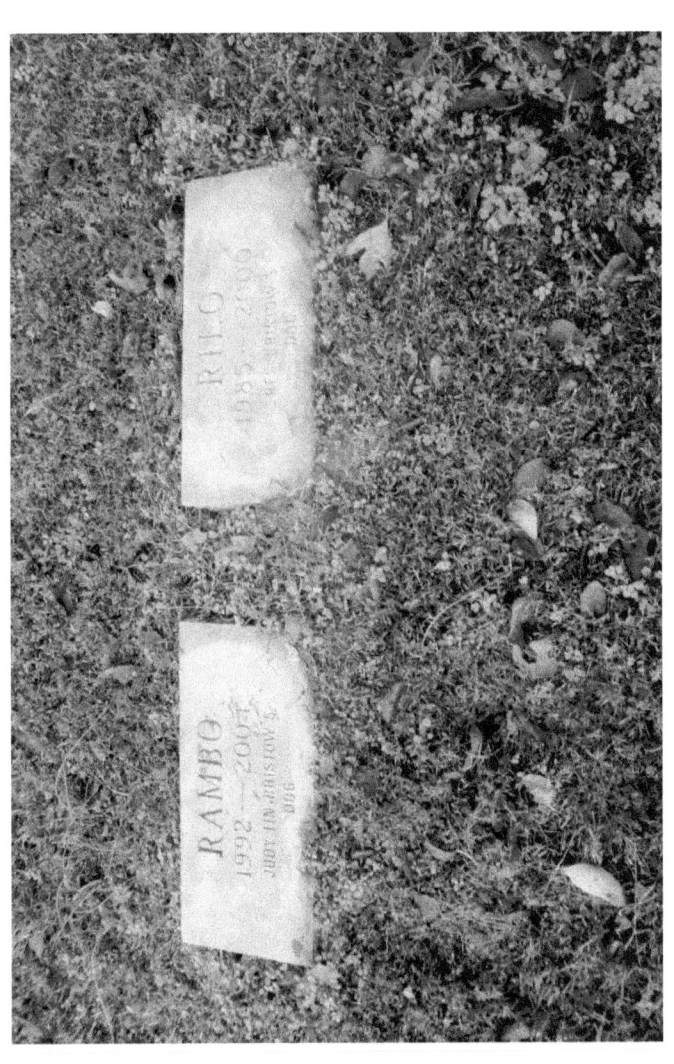

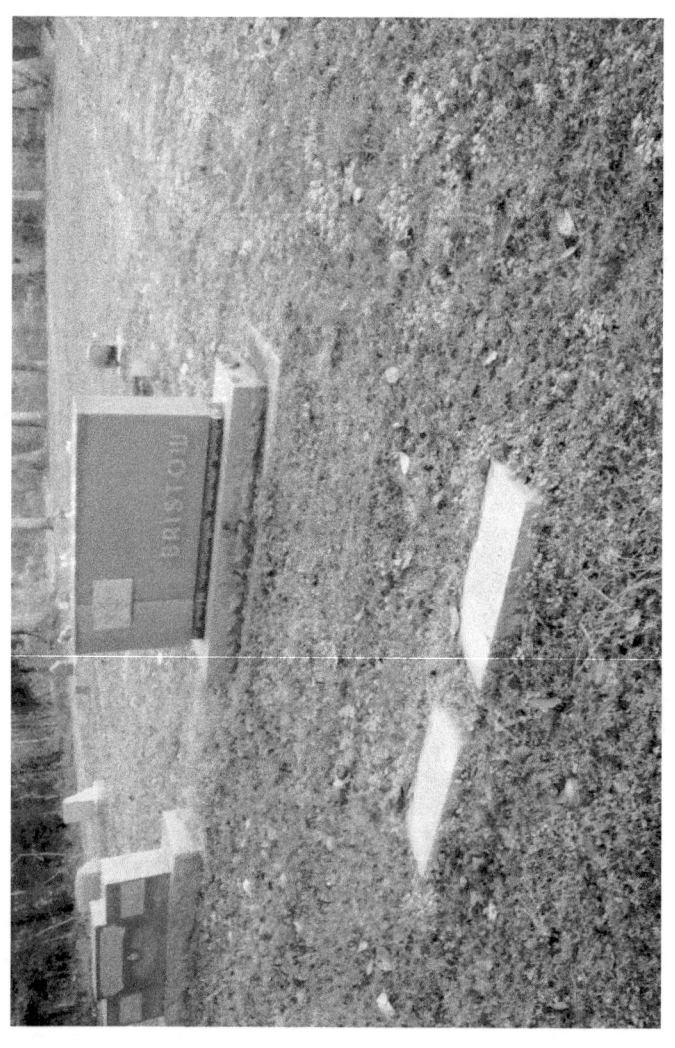

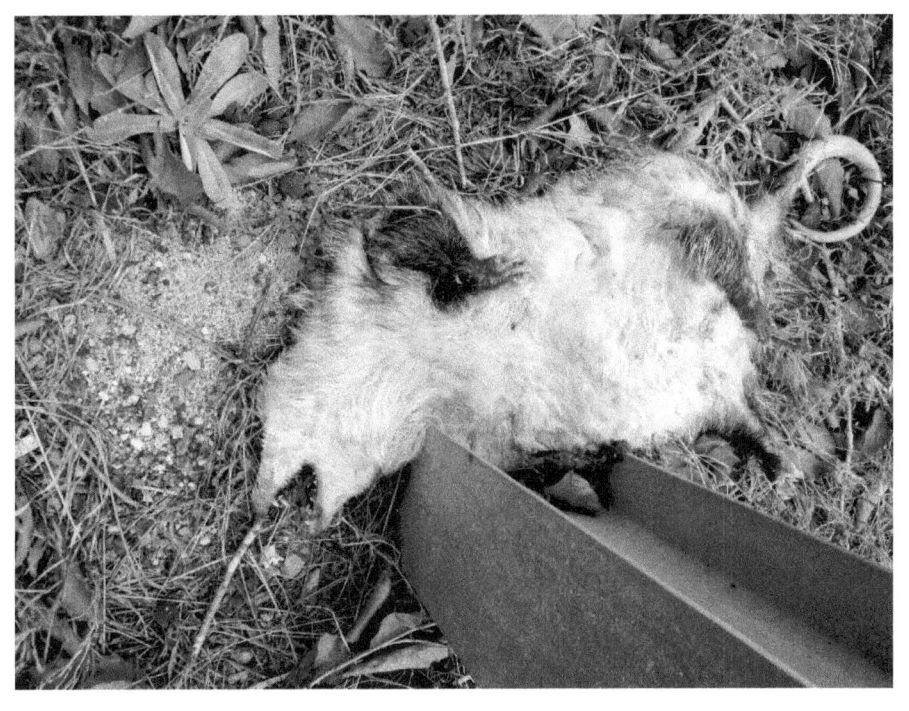

END OF VOLUME 2

www.ingramcontent.com/pod-product-compliance
Lightning Source LLC
Chambersburg PA
CBHW051347170526
45166CB00002B/992